Hooked!

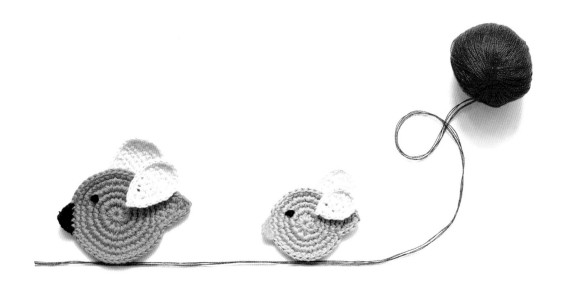

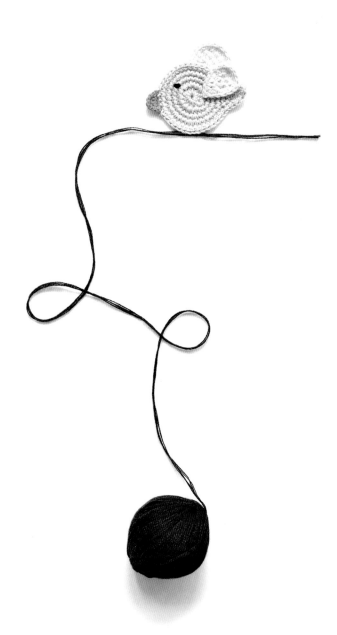

Hooked!

40 Whimsical crochet motifs
from weird to wonderful

MICHELLE, CÉCILE
& SYLVIE DELPRAT

D&C
David and Charles

www.stitchcraftcreate.co.uk

Contents

The Gallery

Michelle, Cécile and Sylvie have created over 40 flowers, appliqués, badges, patches and other fun and bright motifs for you to use to personalise clothing and acessories for you and your family and to give as decorative gifts. Brighten up a little cardigan with a hedgehog for your tiny tot, make a statement of your shopping bag with a crochet badge, give a food lover's key ring to your gourmet friend, or bring to life a plain scarf with bright, floral motifs.

Their playful and quirky creations bring together lavish colour combinations with classic themes inspired by their travels to countries such as India, nature and everyday life. Let your imagination inspire you to use the motifs to brighten up your life!

Flower Power

Crochet these flowers in lots of bright, zingy colours. Attach them to twigs and small branches for a totally unique flower display.

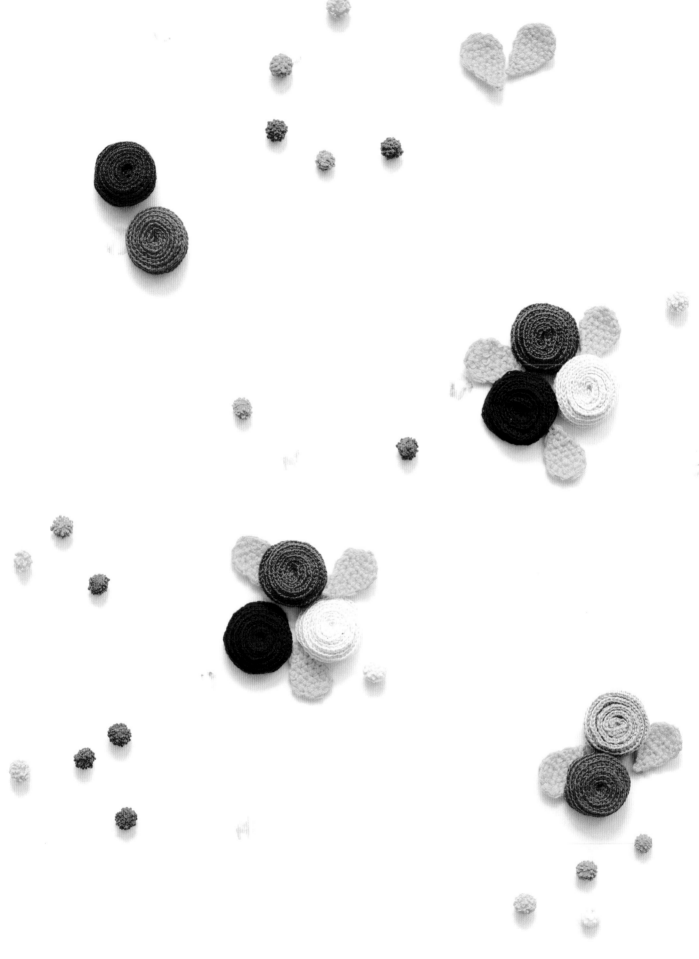

Rose Riot

A simple crocheted rose motif can be used to create a stunning ring or earrings, or group them together to make a bouquet for a brooch or hairclip.

Spread the Red

Attach a bright red motif to a child's cardigan, a hat, a bag, the sleeve
of your jumper or hem of a skirt — where will you put yours?

Love Hearts

Everyone loves a heart — make a practical pin cushion or send one in a card to a
special person on Valentine's Day. Whatever you do, surround yourself with love!

Christmas Joy

A delightful selection of Christmas decorations to add extra cheer to your festivities. Mix and match — anything goes!

Spring is Sprung

Add one of these pretty motifs to a basket, jacket lapel or hat to put a spring in your step.

Top Star

A single star or several stars overlapping will
add a dash of magic to whatever they touch.

Mad Mix

Add a bow tie to a skull, create a bagful of candy or mix
a sunny face with a lightning bolt – who says you can't!

Perfect Bunch

These hot-house flower heads look great bunched together as a striking scarf trim.

Magic Menagerie

Use acid colours and simple shapes to create a cute and whimsical collection of feathered and furry friends. And wait for the snail!

Cute Cupcakes

Who doesn't love a cupcake! Make a whole batch and surround yourself with sweetness.

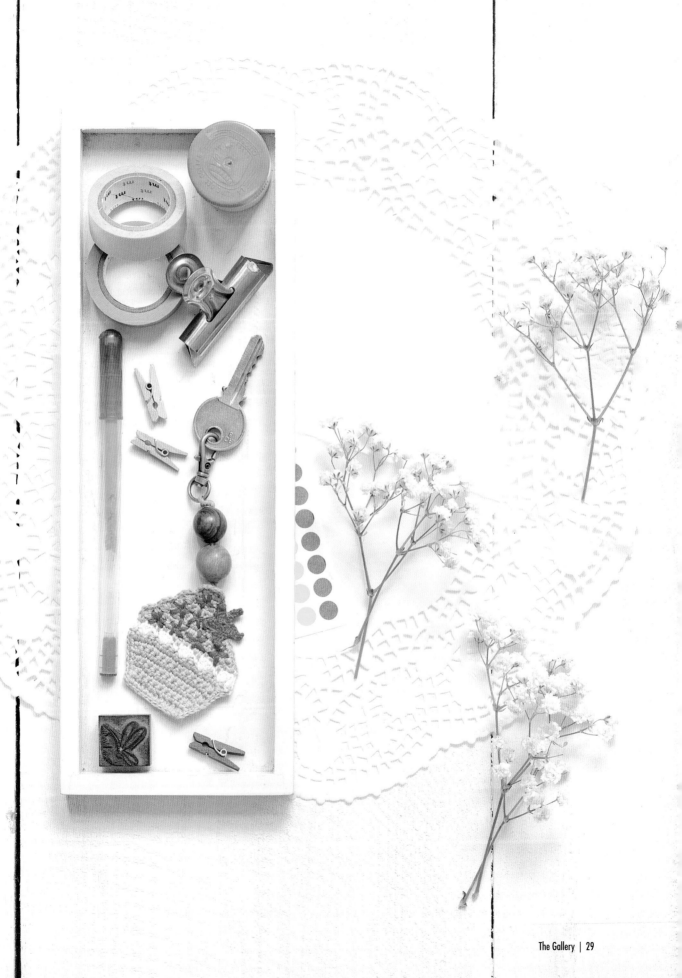

Feathered Friends

In a flap over gift ideas? Check out this flock of fabulous birds —
make a very special one or a whole nestful...

Sleepy Sheep

This smiley sheep is perfect as a mobile or dream catcher to help you on your way to the land of nod and sweet dreams.

Getting Started

Now you've been inspired by The Gallery, get crocheting — choose
your yarn, grab a hook and pick a design or several. The easy-to-follow
patterns will help you create a collection of amazing motifs to use as
gifts, fashion accessories and fun household features. For extra help,
check out the Basic Stitches guide within this chapter and the Conversion
Charts at the back of the book. Most importantly, remember Michelle,
Cécile and Sylvie's simple motto: always crochet with a passion!

A few tips before you start

1. Read the label carefully on the ball of yarn (composition, length, weight, recommended size of crochet hook and care instructions) and refer to the Materials section to check that your yarn is suitable for the motif you want to make.

2. Before starting, always check your tension, making a sample to ensure that your yarn and crochet hook are suitable and that your measurements match those given in the instructions.

3. Instructions given between two asterisks (*) indicate stitches that need to be repeated.

4. The loop on the hook is never counted as a stitch.

5. Read all the pattern instructions in full before starting, to be sure you have understood them all.

6. Always insert the hook into the work from front to back, unless indicated otherwise.

7. Always insert the hook under the two loops at the top of the stitches, unless indicated otherwise.

8. There should always be one loop remaining on the hook once a stitch has been completed, unless indicated otherwise.

9. Begin every row by inserting the hook as indicated into the turning chain stitches.

10. Always block your motif following the instructions on the yarn ball band.

11. Have fun! Change the colours and materials used in the motifs, follow your own instincts and style, and make the designs your own.

Basic Stitches

There are only a few basic crochet stitches and they're easy to master. To achieve work with an even finish, do not pull the yarn too tightly, so you can draw the hook through the loops easily and always maintain the same tension. All patterns in this book use abbreviations for the stitch names and other key crochet terms — a list of abbreviations and their meanings are in the Conversion Charts section. Please note that UK crochet terms are used throughout. The Conversion Charts section lists the UK terms with their US equivalent.

CHAIN (ABBREVIATION – CH)

1. Make a slipknot by wrapping the yarn around the hook, then drawing it through the loop.

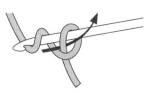

2. To form a chain, take the yarn over the hook (take the yarn from the back over the hook to the front) and draw through the loop.

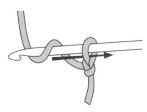

3. Repeat stage 2 until you have the required number of stitches. The loop on the hook is not counted as a stitch. The drawing below shows a chain made up of 4 chain stitches.

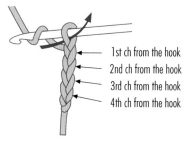

1st ch from the hook
2nd ch from the hook
3rd ch from the hook
4th ch from the hook

SLIP STITCH (ABBREVIATION – SS)

1. Make a foundation chain. Insert the hook into the stitch indicated in the instructions.

2. Yarn over hook and draw the yarn through both loops. One loop remains on the hook.

DOUBLE CROCHET (ABBREVIATION – DC)

1. Make a foundation chain. Insert the hook into the 2nd stitch from the hook (or into the stitch indicated in the instructions).

2. Yarn over hook and draw the yarn through one loop. Two loops remain on the hook.

3. Yarn over hook and draw the yarn through both loops. One loop remains on the hook.

HALF TREBLE (ABBREVIATION – HTR)

1. Make a foundation chain. Yarn over and insert the hook into the 3rd stitch from the hook (or into the stitch indicated in the instructions).

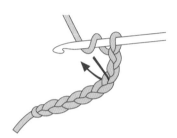

2. Yarn over hook and draw the yarn through one loop. Three loops remain on the hook.

3. Yarn over hook. Draw the yarn through three loops. One loop remains on the hook.

TREBLE (ABBREVIATION – TR)

1. Make a foundation chain. Yarn over and insert the hook into the 4th stitch from the hook (or into the stitch indicated in the instructions).

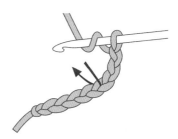

2. Yarn over hook and draw the yarn through one loop. Three loops remain on the hook.

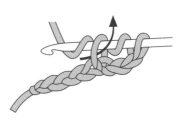

3. Yarn over hook and draw the yarn through the two loops. Two loops remain on the hook.

4. Yarn over hook and draw the yarn through both loops. One loop remains on the hook.

DOUBLE TREBLE (ABBREVIATION – DTR)

1. Make a foundation chain. Bring yarn over the hook twice and insert the hook into the 5th stitch from the hook (or into the stitch indicated within the instructions).

2. Yarn over hook and draw the yarn through one loop. Four loops remain on the hook.

3. Yarn over hook and draw the yarn through two loops. Three loops remain on the hook.

4. Yarn over hook and draw the yarn through two loops. Two loops remain on the hook.

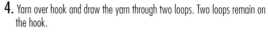

5. Yarn over hook and draw the yarn through two loops. One loop remains on the hook.

Working in Rows

All of the basic crochet stitches can be worked in rows. You generally work from right to left, turning the work at the end of each row.
Working in rows requires you to do 'turning' chain stitches at the beginning of each row (the abbreviation 't-ch' is used to refer to the turning chain in this book), in order to bring the yarn up to the desired height for the stitches starting the row. The turning stitches made at the beginning of the row form the first stitch. Once you get to the start of a row, make the desired number of chain stitches for the first stitch you need to work (unless indicated otherwise).

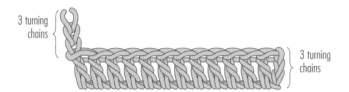

3 turning chains

3 turning chains

NUMBER OF TURNING CHAIN STITCHES NEEDED

BEFORE A:	NO. OF CH
double crochet	1
half treble	2
treble	3
double treble	4
triple treble	5
quadruple treble	6

Magic Ring

To start with an adjustable ring known as a magic ring, wrap the yarn once or twice around your left index finger.
Make the first stitch by inserting the hook into the ring and working a slip stitch to secure. Remove your finger and continue to work as instructed, inserting the hook into the loop. Then pull on the yarn tail to draw the ring tight.

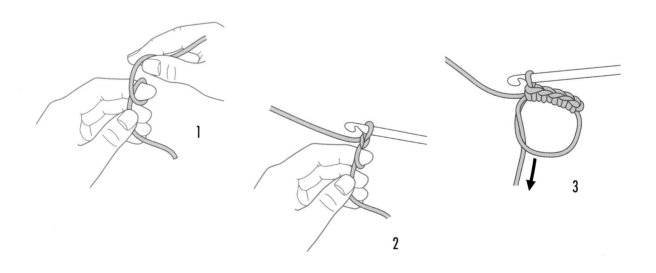

1

2

3

Joining New Colours

When you're about to change colours, work until there are two loops left on your hook. Leaving a tail, draw the end of the new colour through the two loops on the hook. Continue in the pattern with the new ball of yarn. Once complete, weave in the tails of both colours to secure.

1

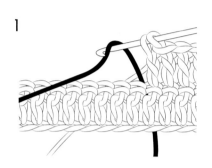

2

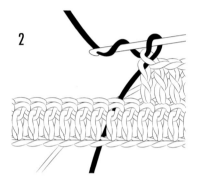

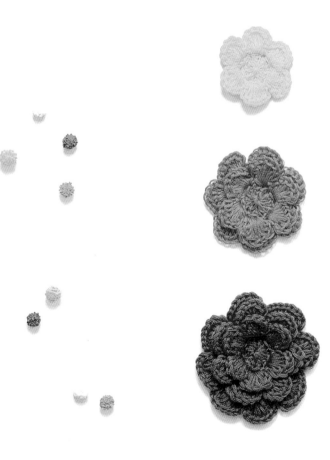

The Patterns

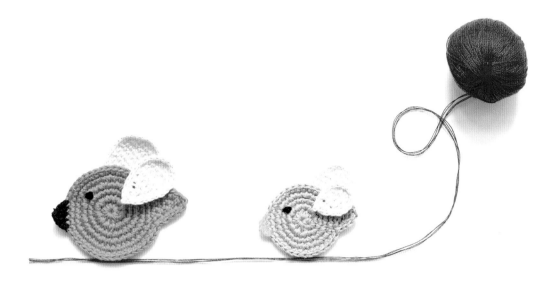

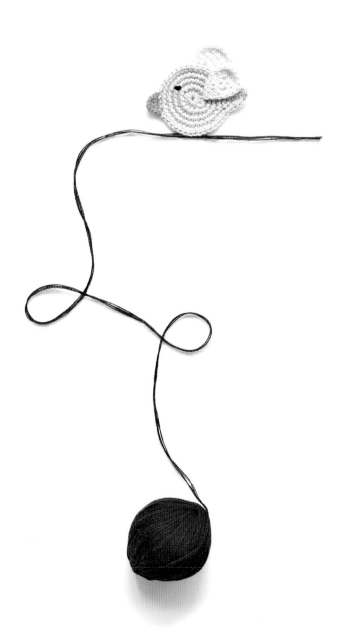

Sunflower

YOU WILL NEED
50g (1¾oz) – 140m (153yds) of 100% cotton yarn in yellow
50g (1¾oz) – 140m (153yds) of 100% cotton yarn in orange
50g (1¾oz) – 140m (153yds) of 100% cotton yarn in brown
2mm (US 4) crochet hook
1 removable stitch marker
SIZE: 7.5cm (3in) in diameter
TENSION: Work 3 sts and 2 rows of htr to measure 1cm (½in) square

INSTRUCTIONS

Start with a magic ring. Crochet in a continual spiral, without closing the previous round. Use a marker to indicate the start of each round, moving it as the work progresses.

Rnd 1: make a magic ring using orange cotton, 2 ch (counts as 1 htr), 7 htr in ring, pull on yarn tail to close up the ring, ss in 2nd ch of t-ch to join (8 sts)

Rnd 2 (inc.): 2 htr in each st on previous rnd, ss in 2nd ch of t-ch to join. Fasten off and weave in ends (16 sts)

Join brown cotton.

Rnd 3 (inc.): 1 dc, *2 dc, 2 dc in next st*, repeat from * to * four times, ss to first dc of round to join (21 sts)

Rnd 4 (inc.): *1 dc, 3 ch, miss 2 dc*, repeat from * to * six times, ss to first dc to join. Fasten off and weave in ends (6 ch-sps)

Join yellow cotton.

Rnd 5 (inc.): insert hook into first ch-sp, 3 ch (counts as 1 tr), 6 dtr, 1 tr, 1 htr in same ch-sp, work 1 tr, 6 dtr, 1 tr, 1 htr in each ch-sp around, ss in 3rd ch of t-ch to join

Rnd 6: *4 htr, (2 htr, 1 ch, 2 htr) in next dtr, 4 htr, 1 dc between next 2 sts*, repeat from * to * six times. Fasten off and weave in ends (6 petals worked)

TIP

To create a pretty summer bouquet, make several sunflowers, playing with different combinations of the three colours. Get a little piece of a branch and hang each of the flowers from the tips, using a piece of wire.

Rose

YOU WILL NEED

50 (1¾oz) – 140m (153yds) of 100% cotton yarn in pink

0.75mm (US 14) crochet hook

Tapestry needle

SIZE: 2.5cm (1in) in diameter

TENSION: Work 10 sts to measure 1cm (½in) wide

INSTRUCTIONS

Work back and forth in rows.

Make a foundation chain of 234 ch.

Row 1: 1 dtr in 5th ch from hook, 4 dtr, *1 dtr, 1 ch, miss 1 ch, (1 dtr, 1 ch, 1 dtr) in next ch, 1 ch, miss 1 ch, 1 dtr, 1 ch, miss 1 ch, (1 dtr, 1 ch) three times in next ch,*, repeat from * to * along entire length of the foundation chain

Row 2: 1 dc in each dtr and each ch-sp in previous row. Fasten off and weave in ends

FINISHING OFF

Draw up the strip you have made by passing a length of yarn through the foundation chain: start at the base sts for the dtr at the beginning and gradually stitch the strip together by sewing small, even, running stitches in the foundation chain, forming a circular shape.

Finish by pushing the point formed by the first dtr clusters on the round into the centre of the rose using the rounded end of the crochet hook.

Fasten off and weave in ends.

TIP

If you use a fine yarn for making this rose, you could easily turn it into a ring. Put a spot of fabric glue on a ring blank and affix the rose by pressing it in place slightly to ensure it sticks perfectly. Leave it to dry and it's done!

Leaf

YOU WILL NEED

50g (1¾oz) 140m (153yds) 100% cotton yarn in green
1.25mm (US 10) crochet hook
1 removable stitch marker
SIZE: 1.5 x 2cm (⅝ x ¾in)
TENSION: Work 5 sts and 5 dc to measure 1cm (½in) square

INSTRUCTIONS

Work back and forth in rows.
Row 1: 3 ch, 2 htr in 3rd ch from hook, turn.
Row 2: 2 htr in each st across, turn. (6 sts)
Rows 3–4: htr across, turn (6 sts)
Row 5: 4 htr, htr2tog, turn (5 sts)
Row 6: 3 htr, htr2tog, turn (4 sts)
Row 7: 2 htr, htr2tog, turn (3 sts)
Row 8: 2 htr
Fasten off and weave in ends.

FINISHING OFF

With RS facing, insert the hook into the first ch that you started with, 1 ch, 1 dc in each stitch/row around. ss to first dc to join. Fasten off and weave in ends.

Pear

YOU WILL NEED

50g (1¾oz) – 140m (153yds) 100% cotton yarn in green
50g (1¾oz) – 140m (153yds) 100% cotton yarn in white
50g (1¾oz) – 140m (153yds) 100% cotton yarn in red
1 skein of white cotton embroidery floss
2mm (US 4) crochet hook
1 removable stitch marker
Tapestry needle
SIZE: 3.5 x 6.5cm (1¼ x 2½in)
TENSION: Work 3 sts and 2 rows of htr to measure 1cm (½in) square

INSTRUCTIONS

Start with a magic ring. Crochet in a continual spiral, without closing the previous round. Use a marker to indicate the start of each round, moving it as the work progresses.

PEAR

Rnd 1: make a magic ring using red cotton, ss to secure. 3 ch (counts as 1 htr), 11 htr in ring, pull on tail to close up the ring (12 sts)
Rnd 2: 2 htr in each st around (24 sts)
Rnd 3: htr around (24 sts)
Crochet the top section of the pear, working back and forth in rows as follows:
Row 1: 5 htr, turn
Row 2: 5 htr
Fasten off and weave in ends.

EDGING

With RS facing, join white yarn and dc evenly around.

STALK

Continue using white cotton and insert hook between 2 dc at top of pear, 7 ch, 1 htr in the 3rd ch from hook, 3 htr, 1 dc, ss in the dc at base of stalk. Fasten off and weave in ends.

LEAF

Join green cotton to the first dc of the stalk. Work back and forth in rows as follows:
Row 1: 3 ch, 2 tr in the dc at start of the stalk, turn (3 sts)
Row 2: 2 ch, 1 htr in base of ch, 1 htr, 2 htr in the last st (5 sts)
Row 3: 2 ch, 1 htr in base of ch, 3 htr, 2 htr in last st (7 sts)
Row 4: 2 ch, htr2tog, 2 htr, htr2tog (5 sts)
Row 5: 2 ch, htr2tog, htr2tog (3 sts)
Row 6: 2 ch, htr2tog
Fasten off and weave in ends.

EMBROIDERY

Embroider a vertical line down the centre of the pear in stem stitch, using three strands of white embroidery floss and a circle at the base, using two strands of embroidery floss.

Simple Flower

YOU WILL NEED
50g (1¾oz) – 140m (153yds) of 100% cotton yarn in white
50g (1¾oz) – 140m (153yds) of 100% cotton yarn in red
2mm (US 4) crochet hook
1 removable stitch marker
Tapestry needle
SIZE: 4cm (1½in) diameter
TENSION: Work 3 sts and 1 row of htr to measure 1cm (½in) square

INSTRUCTIONS

Start with a magic ring. Crochet in a continual spiral, without closing the previous round. Use a marker to indicate the start of each round, moving it as the work progresses.

THE CENTRE

Rnd 1: make a magic ring using off-white cotton yarn, ss to secure. 3 ch (counts as 1 tr), 11 tr in ring, ss in 3rd ch of t-ch to join. Pull tail to close up ring (12 sts)

Rnd 2: (inc): *1 dc, 2 ch, miss 1 tr *; repeat from * to * five more times
Fasten off and weave in ends.

PETALS

Join red cotton to any 2 ch-sp from previous rnd. Work (1 dc, 1 htr, 4 tr, 1 htr) in each 2 ch-sp around, ss in first dc to join. Fasten off and weave in ends.

TIP

This is one of the simplest and quickest flowers to crochet, so it's perfect for beginners. Not only can you have fun with the colours by making the centre and petals out of various shades, but you can also try using other materials besides cotton for a different effect.

Cherries

YOU WILL NEED

50g (1¾oz) — 140m (153yds) of 100% cotton yarn in red
50g (1¾oz) — 140m (153yds) of 100% cotton yarn in brown
50g (1¾oz) — 140m (153yds) of 100% cotton yarn in green
1.25mm crochet hook (please note that there is no US crochet hook size equivalent for this size. The closest is a US 10)
1.5mm (US 8) crochet hook
1 removable stitch marker
Tapestry needle
SIZE: 2.5 x 6.5cm (1 x 2⅝ in)
TENSION: Work 4 sts and 4 rows of dc to measure 1cm (½in) square

INSTRUCTIONS

Start with a magic ring. Crochet in a continual spiral, without closing the previous round. Use a marker to indicate the start of each round, moving it as the work progresses.

CHERRY

(make 2)

Rnd 1: using red cotton and the 1.25mm hook, make a magic ring and ss to secure. 2 ch (counts as 1 htr), 9 htr in ring, pull on tail to close the ring. (10 sts)

Rnd 2: *2 dc in next st, 2 dc*, rep from * to * twice more, 1 dc in next st. (13 sts)

Rnd 3: *2 dc in next st, 3 dc*, rep from * to * twice more, 2 dc in last st. (17 sts)

Rnd 4: 2 dc in next st, 1 dc in each st to end. ss to first dc to join

Fasten off and weave in ends. Repeat for second cherry.

STALKS

Using brown cotton and a 1.5mm (US 8) hook, join the yarn at any point on the edge of a cherry. Work 1 dc and 15 ch.

Turn, and work 1 dc in each of the next 5 ch of previous stalk, 9 ch, ss to desired point on edge of second cherry.

Fasten off and weave in ends.

LEAF

Using green cotton and a 1.25mm hook, join yarn to 5th dc of stalk and work as follows:

Row 1: 2 ch, 2 htr in the 4 th dc, 1 htr in the next dc (4 sts)

Row 2: 2 ch, 2 htr in the next st, 1 htr, 2 htr in the last st (6 sts)

Row 3: 2 ch, 2 htr in the next st, 3 htr, 2 htr in the last st (8 sts)

Row 4: 2 ch, 2 htr in the next st, 6 htr (9 sts)

Row 5: 2 ch, 8 htr (9 sts)

Row 6: 2 ch, htr2tog, 4 htr, htr2tog (7 sts)

Row 7: 2 ch, htr2tog, 2 htr, htr2tog (5 sts)

Row 8: 2 ch, 4 htr (5 sts)

Row 9: 2 ch, 3 htr (4 sts)

Row 10: 2 ch, 2 htr (3 sts)

Row 11: 2 ch, 1 htr (2 sts)

Fasten off, leaving a long tail.

Thread needle with the tail. Work a running stitch around the edge, pulling it slightly tight.

Fasten off and weave in ends.

Toadstool

YOU WILL NEED
50g (1¾oz) – 140m (153yds) of 100% cotton yarn in red
1 skein of white cotton embroidery floss
2mm (US 4) crochet hook
Tapestry needle
SIZE: 4 x 5cm (1½ x 2in)
TENSION: Work 3 sts and 2 rows of htr to measure 1cm (½in) square

INSTRUCTIONS

CAP
Work back and forth in rows.
Row 1: with red cotton, 12 ch, 1 htr in 3rd ch from hook and in each ch across, turn (11 sts)
Row 2: 2 ch, htr across (11 sts)
Row 3: 2 ch, htr2tog, 6 htr, htr2tog, turn (9 sts)
Row 4: 2 ch, htr2tog, 4 htr, htr2tog, turn (7 sts)
Row 5: 2 ch, 6 htr
Fasten off, leaving a long tail.

EDGING
Using the long tail, 1ch, work a row of dc evenly around, ss to first dc to join.
Fasten off and weave in ends.

STALK
With the RS of the Toadstool Cap facing, and working into the bottom, join the off-white cotton to the 4th st from the side and work as follows:.
Row 1: 2 ch, 4 htr, turn (5 sts)
Row 2: 2 ch, 4 htr, turn (5 sts)
Row 3: 2 ch, 1 htr, 2 htr in next st, 1 htr, 2 htr in the last st (7 sts)
Row 4: 2 ch, 2 htr in the next st, 5 htr (8 sts)
Row 5: 2 ch, 7 htr (8 sts)
Fasten off and weave in ends.
Re-join the off-white yarn to the top of the stalk (where it meets the Cap), 1 ch, dc evenly around the edge. ss to base of Cap to join. Fasten off and weave in ends.

EMBROIDERY
Using the tapestry needle, embroider nine little dots in satin stitch, using two strands of white embroidery floss.

Strawberry

YOU WILL NEED

50G (1¾OZ) – 140M (153YDS) OF 100% COTTON YARN IN RED
50g (1¾oz) – 140m (153yds) of 100% cotton yarn in green
2mm (US 4) crochet hook
1.25mm crochet hook (please note that there is no US crochet hook size equivalent for this size. The closest is a US 10)
Tapestry needle
SIZE: 3 x 4.5cm (1¼ x 1¾in)
TENSION: Work 3 sts and 3 rows of dc to measure 1cm (½in) square

INSTRUCTIONS

STRAWBERRY

Using red cotton and a 2mm (US 4) hook, work back and forth in rows as follows:
Row 1: 2 ch, 3 dc in 2nd ch from hook, turn (3 sts)
Row 2: 1 ch, 2 dc in first st, 1 dc, 2 dc in the last st (5 sts)
Row 3: 1 ch, 2 dc in first st, 3 dc, 2 dc in the last st (7 sts)
Row 4: 1 ch, 2 dc in the first st, 6dc (8 sts)
Row 5: 1 ch, 2 dc in the first st, 7 dc (9 sts)
Row 6: 1 ch, dc across (9 sts)
Row 7: 1 ch, miss first st, 6 dc, dc2tog (7 sts)
Row 8: 1 ch, miss first st, 4 dc, dc2tog (5 sts)
Row 9: 1 ch, dc across (5 sts)
Fasten off, leaving a long tail.
Use tail to dc evenly around the edge, ss to first dc to join.
Fasten off, weave in ends.

LEAF

Using green cotton and 1.25mm crochet hook, work in the round as follows:
Rnd 1: 3 ch (counts as 1 htr), 8 htr in 3rd ch from hook, ss to 3rd ch of t-ch to join (9 sts)
Rnd 2: 1 ch, 9 dc, ss to first dc to join (9 sts)
Rnd 3: *5 ch, insert hook into 2nd ch from hook, 1 dc, 3 htr, skip 1 dc on Round 2 and work 1 dc in next dc*, rep from * to * three more times (4 rounds)
Do not fasten off, but continue to work the Stalk as follows:

STALK

7 ch, insert hook into the 3rd ch from hook, 4 htr, 1dc, ss to first ch of next frond.
Fasten off and weave in ends.

FINISHING

Use the tapestry needle and green cotton to attach the leaf to the top of the strawberry, with the stalk facing upwards.

Hedgehog

YOU WILL NEED

50g (1¾oz) – 140m (153yds) of 100% cotton yarn in red
50g (1¾oz) – 140m (153yds) of 100% cotton yarn in off-white
1 skein of black cotton embroidery floss
2mm (US 4) crochet hook
1 removable stitch marker
Tapestry needle
SIZE: 7 x 5cm (2¾ x 2in)
TENSION: Work 5 sts and 3 rows of htr to measure 1cm (½in) square

INSTRUCTIONS

Start with a magic ring. Crochet in a continual spiral, without closing the previous round. Use a marker to indicate the start of each round, moving it as the work progresses.

BODY

Rnd 1: make a magic ring using red cotton, ss to secure, 2 ch (counts as 1 htr), 10 htr in ring, pull on tail to close the ring (11 sts)
Rnd 2: 2 htr in each st around (22 sts)
Rnd 3: htr around (22 sts)
Rnd 4: *2 htr in next st, 1 htr*, rep from * to * ten more times (32 sts).

SPIKES

*(1 dc, 2 ch, 1 htr, 2 ch, 1 dc) in next st, 1 dc; rep from * to * six more times, ss in next st. Fasten off and weave in ends.

HEAD

Using off-white yarn, insert hook into the next st after the last spine worked.
Row 1: 2 ch, 6 htr, turn (7 sts)
Row 2: 2 ch, 6 htr, turn (7 sts)

Row 3: 2 ch, 5 htr, turn (6 sts)
Row 4: 2 ch, 4 htr, turn (5 sts)
Row 5: 2 ch, 3 htr, turn (4 sts)
Row 6: 2 ch, 2 htr
Fasten off, leaving a long tail.
Using long tail, 1 ch, dc evenly around head, ss to joining st on body to secure.
Fasten off and weave in ends.

EMBROIDERY

For the eye, embroider a little dot in satin stitch, using two strands of embroidery floss.
Using three strands of embroidery floss, work in long stitch for the snout.

Apple

YOU WILL NEED
50g (1¾oz) – 140m (153yds) of 100% cotton yarn in off-white
50g (1¾oz) – 140m (153yds) of 100% cotton yarn in green
1 skein of white cotton embroidery floss
2mm (US 4) crochet hook
1 removable stitch marker
Tapestry needle
SIZE: 3.5 x 5.5cm (1½ x 2¼in)
TENSION: Work 3 sts and 2 rows of htr to measure 1cm (½in) square

INSTRUCTIONS

APPLE

Start with a magic ring. Crochet in a continual spiral, without closing the previous round. Use a marker to indicate the start of each round, moving it as the work progresses.

Rnd 1: using red cotton, make a magic ring and ss to secure. 2 ch (counts as 1 htr), 11 htr in ring. Pull on tail to close the ring (12 sts)
Rnd 2: (inc): 2 htr in each st around (24 sts)
Rnd 3: 2 htr in next st, htr around (25 sts)
Fasten off and weave in ends.
Join off-white yarn to any edge stitch, 2 ch, dc evenly around the apple edge, ss to first dc to secure.
Fasten off and weave in ends.

STALK

Using off-white cotton, insert hook to the top of the apple, 7 ch, 1 htr in 3rd ch from hook, 3 htr, 1 dc, ss in dc at apple edge to secure.
Fasten off and weave in ends.

LEAF

Join green cotton to the first dc of the stalk. Work back and forth in rows as follows:
Row 1: 3 ch, 2 tr in the dc at start of the stalk, turn (3 sts)
Row 2: 2 ch, 1 htr in base of ch, 1 htr, 2 htr in the last st (5 sts)
Row 3: 2 ch, 1 htr in base of ch, 3 htr, 2 htr in last st (7 sts)
Row 4: 2 ch, htr2tog, 2htr, htr2tog (5 sts)
Row 5: 2 ch, htr2tog, htr2tog (3 sts)
Row 6: 2 ch, htr2tog
Fasten off and weave in ends.

EMBROIDERY

Using three strands of embroidery floss, embroider a vertical line down the middle of the apple in stem stitch, and a ring in the centre.

Heart

YOU WILL NEED
50g (1¾oz) — 140m (153yds) of 100% cotton yarn in pink
2mm (US 4) crochet hook
SIZE: 4 x 4cm (1½ x 1½in)
TENSION: Work 4 sts and 3 rows of htr to measure 1cm (½in) square

INSTRUCTIONS

Row 1: 3 ch, 2 htr in 3rd ch from hook, turn (3 sts)

Row 2: 2 ch, 1 htr in base of ch, 2 htr in each st across, turn (6 sts)

Row 3: 2 ch, 1 htr in base of ch, 4 htr, 2 htr in the last st, turn (8 sts)

Row 4: 2 ch, 1 htr in base of ch, 6 htr, 2htr in the last st, turn (10 sts)

Row 5: 2 ch, 1 htr in base of ch, 8 htr, 2 htr in the last st, turn (12 sts)

Row 6: 2 ch, 1 htr in base of ch, 10 htr, 2htr in the last st, turn (14 sts)

Row 7: 2 ch, htr across, turn

SHAPING:

Row 8: 2 ch, 6 htr, turn (7 sts)

Row 9: 2 ch, 5 htr, turn (6 sts)

Row 10: 2 ch, miss first st, 4 htr (5 sts)

Fasten off.

Rejoin yarn to right side at Row 8 (half of this row has already been done) at the 8th st. Rep Rows 8–10.

Fasten off, leaving a long tail.

FINISHING OFF

Using long tail, 1 ch, dc evenly around the edge, ss to first dc to join.

Fasten off and weave in ends.

TIP
_____

It's simple to turn this motif into a pin cushion (see photo page). You just use thicker wool. Make a sample before starting to ensure you get two hearts measuring about 8 x 8cm (3¼ x 3¼in). Seam together, leaving an opening. Stuff, then sew up the opening.

Candy Cane

YOU WILL NEED

50g (1¾oz) – 140m (153yds) of 100% cotton yarn in off-white
50g (1¾oz) – 140m (153yds) of 100% cotton yarn in red
1mm (US 12) crochet hook
SIZE: 1 x 6cm (½ x 2½in)
TENSION: Work 5 sts and 3 rows of tr to measure 1cm (½in) square

INSTRUCTIONS

Change shades every two rows by working the last 'yarn round hook' with the other shade.

Row 1: using red cotton, 3 ch, 2 dc in 2nd ch from hook, 2 dc in last ch, turn (4 sts)

Row 2: 1 ch, dc across, changing to white in the last st, turn (4 sts)

Row 3: 2 ch, 1 dc in 2nd ch from hook, 2 dc, dc2tog, turn (4 sts)

Row 4: 1 ch, 4 dc, change to red in the last st, turn (4 sts)

Row 5: 2 ch, 1 dc in 2nd ch from hook, 2 dc, dc2tog, turn (4 sts)

Row 6: 1ch, 4 dc, change to white in the last st, turn. (4 sts)

Rows 7–16: repeat rows 3–6, ending on a row 4

Row 17: 1 ch, 2 dc, 2 htr in next st, 1 tr in last st, turn (5 sts)

Row 18: 2 ch, 1htr, 2htr in next st, 2 htr, changing to white in last st, turn (6 sts)

Row 19: 1 ch, miss next st, 4 tr in next st, miss next st, ss to last st, turn

Row 20: 2 ch, miss next st, 4 dc; change to red and work 1 dc in first st of row 18 before turning the work, turn

Row 21: 1 dc, 3 htr, turn

Row 22: 1 ch, 1 dc, 3 dc in next st, 1 dc, changing to white in the last st, turn

Row 23: 2 ch, 4 tr in next st, skip 2 sts, 1 dc in next st

Fasten off and weave in ends.

FINISHING OFF

Rejoin red cotton to any edge stitch, 1 ch, work dcs evenly around the edge, ss to first dc to join.

Fasten off and weave in ends.

Angel

YOU WILL NEED
50g (1¾oz) – 140m (153yds) of 100% cotton yarn in off-white
1 length of blue and 1 length of brown embroidery floss
1mm (US 12) crochet hook.
Tapestry needle
SIZE: 5 x 6cm (2 x 2½in)
TENSION: Work 5 sts and 3 rows of htr to measure 1cm (½in) square

INSTRUCTIONS

DRESS
Row 1: 22 ch, 1 htr in 3rd ch from hook, htr in each ch across, turn (20 sts)

Rows 2–4: 2 ch, htr across, turn (20 sts)

Row 5: 2 ch, 17 htr, htr2tog, turn (19 sts)

Row 6: 2 ch, 16 htr, htr2tog, turn (18 sts)

Row 7: 2 ch, 15 htr, htr2tog, turn (17 sts)

Row 8: 2 ch, 14 htr, htr2tog, turn (16 sts)

Row 9: 2 ch, 13 htr, htr2tog, turn (15 sts)

Row 10: 2 ch, 12 htr, htr2tog, turn (14 sts)

Row 11: 2 ch, 11 htr, htr2tog, turn (13 sts)

Row 12: 2 ch, 10 htr, htr2tog, turn (12 sts)

Row 13: 2 ch, 9 htr, htr2tog, turn (11 sts)

Row 14: 2 ch, 8 htr, htr2tog, turn (10 sts)

Row 15: 2 ch, 7 htr, htr2tog, turn (9 sts)

HEAD
Row 16: 2 ch, 2 htr in next st, 6 htr, 2 htr in last st (11 sts)

Rows 18–19: 2 ch, 10 htr (11 sts)

Row 20: 2 ch, htr2tog, 6 htr, htr2tog (9 sts)

Row 21: 2 ch, htr2tog, 4 htr, htr2tog (7 sts)

Row 22: 2 ch, htr2tog, 2 htr, htr2tog (5 sts)
Fasten off and weave in ends.

OUTLINE OF HEAD
Rejoin off-white cotton to the base of the head (at row 15 of body), 1 ch, dc evenly around the head to the other side. Fasten off and weave in ends.

WINGS
Using white cotton, and with RS facing, rejoin yarn in first edge st on Row 13. Crochet back down the body, working into the sides of the stitches, as follows:

Row 1: 2 ch, 1 htr at base of ch, 2 htr each in side of Rows 14 and 15 of body (6 sts)

Row 2: 2 ch, 2 htr in next st, 3 htr, 2 htr in last st (8 sts)

Row 3: 2 ch, 2 htr in next st, 5 htr, 2 htr in last st (10 sts)

Row 4: 2 ch, 2 htr in next st, 8 htr, 2 htr in last st (12 sts)

Row 5: 1 ch, dc across (12 sts)
Fasten off and weave in ends.
Repeat for the other side.

EMBROIDERY
Embroider the halo in stem stitch, using three strands of brown embroidery floss.
For the eyes, use two strands of blue embroidery floss and embroider in satin stitch.

Gingerbread Man

YOU WILL NEED
50g (1¾oz) – 140m (153yds) of 100% cotton yarn in off-white
1 skein each of brown and red cotton embroidery floss
1mm (US 12) crochet hook
Tapestry needle
SIZE: 4 x 5cm (1½ x 2in)
TENSION: Work 5 sts and 3 rows of htr to measure 1cm (½in) square

INSTRUCTIONS

LEGS AND BODY
Using off-white cotton and starting with the first leg, work as follows:
Row 1: 4 ch, 1 htr in 3rd ch from hook, 2 htr in last ch, turn (4 sts)
Row 2: 2 ch, 2 htr in next st, 1 htr, 2 htr in last st, turn (6 sts)
Row 3: 2 ch, htr across, turn (6 sts)
Row 4: 2 ch, 1 htr in base of ch, htr across, turn (7 sts)
Rows 5–6: 2 ch, htr across, turn
Fasten off.
Make 2nd leg, repeating rows 1 to 6 but do not fasten off. Assemble legs in next row:
Row 7: 2 ch, 6 htr, 7 htr across other leg, turn (14 sts)
Row 8: 2 ch, 4 htr, htr2tog, 5 htr, htr2tog, turn (12 sts)
Row 9: 2 ch, htr2tog, 7 htr, htr2tog, turn (10 sts)
Row 10: 2 ch, htr2tog, 5 htr, htr2tog, turn (8 sts)
Rows 11–12: 2 ch, 7 htr
Fasten off and weave in ends.

ARMS
Row 13: 5 ch using off-white cotton, 8 htr on the top of the body, 5 ch, turn (18 sts)
Row 14: 2 ch, htr in 3rd ch from hook and each ch/st across (18 sts)
Rows 15–17: 2 ch, htr across, turn
Fasten off and weave in ends.

HEAD
Row 18: rejoin yarn at 7th htr on previous row, 2 ch, 2 htr in next two sts, 1 htr, turn (6 sts)
Row 19: 2 ch, 1 htr in base of ch, 4 htr, 2 htr in last st (8 sts)
Row 20: 2 ch, htr across, turn (8 sts)
Row 21: 2 ch, htr2tog, 3 htr, htr2tog (6 sts)
Row 22: 2 ch, htr2tog, 2 htr, htr2tog (4 sts)
Fasten off and weave in ends.

EDGING
Using three strands of brown embroidery floss, join to any edge st, 1 ch, dc evenly around, ss to first dc to join. Fasten off and weave in ends.

BUTTONS
(make 3)
Thread a tapestry needle with three strands of a length of embroidery floss and make a small ring at one end. Pass the needle through the motif to create a small, firm button measuring 0.5cm (¼in) diameter. Sew them onto the gingerbread man, running down the centre of the body.

EMBROIDERY
Embroider the eyes in satin stitch, using two strands of brown embroidery floss.

Flower Head

YOU WILL NEED

50g (1¾oz) – 140m (153yds) of 100% cotton yarn in red
50g (1¾oz) – 140m (153yds) of 100% cotton yarn in brown
50g (1¾oz) – 140m (153yds) of 100% cotton yarn in off-white
1.5mm (US 8) crochet hook
2mm (US 4) crochet hook
1 removable stitch marker
SIZE: 5cm (2in) diameter
TENSION: Work 4 sts and 3 rows of htr to measure 1cm (½in) square

INSTRUCTIONS

Start with a magic ring. Crochet in a continual spiral, without closing the previous round. Use a marker to indicate the start of each round, moving it as the work progresses.

Rnd 1: using a 1.5mm hook and off-white cotton, make a magic ring and ss to secure. 1 ch, 9 dc in ring, pull yarn tail to close the ring (9 sts)

Rnd 2: 2 htr in each st around (18 sts)

Fasten off and weave in ends.

Attach brown cotton to next st.

Rnd 3: dc around, changing to red cotton in last dc (18 dc)

Continue in red cotton.

Rnd 4 (inc.): *2 htr in next st, 1 htr*, rep from * to * eight more times. (27 sts)

Rnd 5: dc around. (27 sts)

FINISHING OFF

Switch to the 2mm (US 4) hook and continue as follows:

5 ch (counts as 1 htr and 3 ch), 1 htr, 3 ch, 1 htr in first st, (1 htr, 3 ch, 1 htr, 3 ch, 1 htr) in each dc around, ss to 3rd ch of t-ch.

Fasten off and weave in ends.

TIP

If crocheted in red and white, the candy cane, angel, gingerbread man and flower head motifs can be turned into cute little Christmas decorations in no time at all. Simply sew a piece of coloured string, folded in two, to the top of each motif.

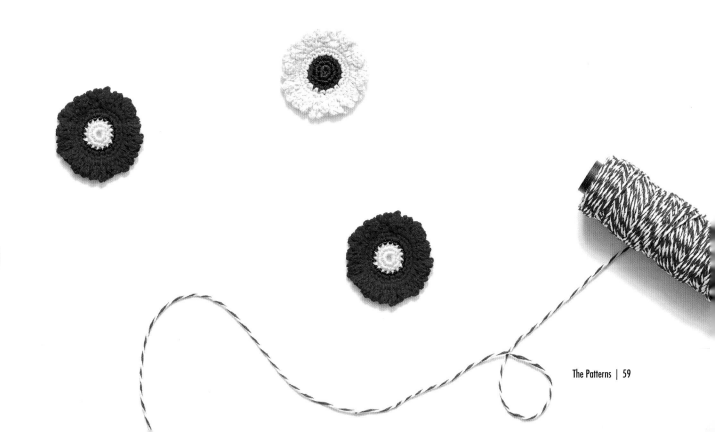

Strawberry Patch

YOU WILL NEED

50g (1¾oz) – 140m (153yds) of 100% cotton yarn in off-white
50g (1¾oz) – 140m (153yds) of 100% cotton yarn in brown
50g (1¾oz) – 140m (153yds) of 100% cotton yarn in black
50g (1¾oz) – 140m (153yds) of 100% cotton yarn in green
50g (1¾oz) – 140m (153yds) of 100% cotton yarn in red
2mm (US 4) crochet hook
1.5mm (US 8) crochet hook
1 removable stitch marker
Tapestry needle
SIZE: 9.5cm (3¾in) diameter
TENSION: Work 3 sts and 2 rows of htr to measure 1cm (½in) square

INSTRUCTIONS

Start with a magic ring. Crochet in a continual spiral, without closing the previous round. Use a marker to indicate the start of each round, moving it as the work progresses.

PATCH

Rnd 1: using brown cotton and a 2mm (US 4) hook, make a magic ring and ss to secure. 2 ch (counts as 1 htr), 8 htr in ring, pull yarn tail to close the ring (9 sts)

Rnd 2 (inc.): 2 htr in each htr around (18 sts)

Rnd 3: *2 dc in next st, 1 dc*, rep from * around (27 sts)

Rnd 4: *2 dc in next st, 2 dc*, rep from * to * around (36 sts)

Rnd 5: *2 dc in next st, 3 dc*, rep from * to * around (45 sts)

Rnd 6: *2 dc in next st, 4 dc*, rep from * to * around (54 sts)

Fasten off and weave in ends.

Join off-white cotton to any dc.

Rnd 7: 2 ch, htr around, ss to 2nd ch of t-ch to join.

Rnd 8: *2 htr in next st, 5 htr*, rep from * to * around (63 sts)

Fasten off and weave in ends.

Join black cotton to any htr.

Rnd 9: 2 ch, htr around, ss to 2nd ch of t-ch to join

Rnd 10: *2 htr in next st, 6 htr*, rep from * to * around (72 sts)

Fasten off and weave in ends.

Join off-white cotton to any htr.

Rnd 11: *1 dc, 1 picot (1 dc, 3 ch and 1 ss worked in the base dc) in the next st*, repeat from * to * around, ss to first dc to join

Fasten off and weave in ends.

STRAWBERRY

Using red cotton and a 1.5mm (US 8) hook, work as follows:

Row 1: 2 ch, 2 dc in 2nd ch from hook, turn (2 sts)

Row 2: 1 ch, 2 dc in each st across, turn (4 sts)

Row 3: 1 ch, 3 dc, 2 dc in last st, turn (5 sts)

Row 4: 1 ch, 4 dc, 2 dc in last st, turn (6 sts)

Row 5: 1 ch, 2 dc in first st, 4 dc, 2 dc in last st, turn (8 sts)

Row 6: 1 ch, 2 dc in first st, 6 dc, 2 dc in last st, turn (10 sts)

Row 7: 1 ch, 10 dc, turn (10 sts)

Row 8: 1 ch, 8 dc, dc2tog, turn (9 sts)

Row 9: 1 ch, dc across, turn. (9 sts)

Row 10: 1 ch, 7 dc, dc2tog, turn (8 sts)

Row 11: 1 ch, 6 dc, dc2tog, turn (7 sts)

Row 12: 1 ch, dc2tog, 3 dc, dc2tog, turn (5 sts)

Row 13: 1 ch, miss first dc, dc2tog twice

Edging: Using red cotton, 1 ch, dc evenly around, ss to first dc to join.

Fasten off and weave in ends.

STALK

Using green yarn and a 1.5mm(US 8) hook, 5 ch, 1 dc in 2nd ch from hook, 1 dc in next ch, 1 htr in next ch, 3 htr in next ch, rotate fabric and work on the other side of the chain as follows: 1 htr, 2 dc, 2 ch, ss in base of first dc.

FRONDS

Continuing from the stalk, *6 ch, 1 trtr (worked by inserting hook in the 2 ch-sp), 6 ch, ss to 2 ch-sp*, rep from * to * twice more.

Fasten off and weave in ends.

Sew the stalk to the top of the strawberry then sew the strawberry to the circular patch.

Rabbit Patch

YOU WILL NEED

50g (1¾oz) — 140m (153yds) of 100% cotton yarn in off-white
50g (1¾oz) — 140m (153yds) of 100% cotton yarn in brown
50g (1¾oz) — 140m (153yds) of 100% cotton yarn in red
50g (1¾oz) — 140m (153yds) of 100% cotton yarn in fawn
1 skein each of black and green Mouliné DMC embroidery floss
1mm (US 12) crochet hook
2mm (US 4) crochet hook
1 removable stitch marker
Tapestry needle
SIZE: 6cm (2½in) diameter
TENSION: Work 3 sts and 2 rows of htr to measure 1cm (½in) square

INSTRUCTIONS

Start with a magic ring. Crochet in a continual spiral, without closing the previous round. Use a marker to indicate the start of each round, moving it as the work progresses.

PATCH

Rnds 1 to 4: work as for the circle for the strawberry patch, using brown cotton and a 2mm (US 4) hook

Fasten off and weave in ends.

Rnd 5: using red cotton, 2 ch, htr around, ss to 2nd ch of t-ch to join

Fasten off and weave in ends.

Rnd 6: using brown cotton, *2 dc in next st, 4 dc*, rep from * to * around (54 sts)

Rnd 7: 1 ch, *1 dc, 1 picot (1 dc, 3 ch and 1 ss worked in the base dc) in the next st*, rep from * to * around, ss in first dc to join

Fasten off and weave in ends.

RABBIT

Using off-white cotton and a 1mm (US 12) hook, work as follows:

Row 1: 10 ch, 1 htr in 3rd ch from hook and in each ch across, turn (8 sts)

Rows 2–3: 2 ch, htr across, turn (8 sts)

Row 4: 2 ch, 5 htr, htr2tog, turn (7 sts)

Row 5: 2 ch, 6 htr, turn (7 sts)

Row 6: 2 ch, 3 htr in base of ch, 4 htr, htr2tog (9 sts)

Row 7: 2 ch, 4 htr, htr2tog (6 sts)

Row 8: 1 ch, dc2tog, 2 htr, dc2tog

Join fawn cotton to 2nd st on previous row, *5 ch, 1 htr in 3rd ch from hook, 1 htr, 1 dc, ss in base of ch*. dc in next st on rabbit, repeat from * to * for 2nd ear.

Fasten off and weave in ends.

Sew the rabbit to the centre of patch.

EMBROIDERY

Make a round shape for the eye using small straight stitches and two strands of black embroidery floss. For the grass, sew vertical straight stitches using three strands of green floss, then embroider a horizontal line in stem stitch along the bottom of the grass.

Cherry Patch

YOU WILL NEED

50g (1¾oz) – 140m (153yds) of 100% cotton yarn in off-white
50g (1¾oz) – 140m (153yds) of 100% cotton yarn in green
50g (1¾oz) – 140m (153yds) of 100% cotton yarn in fawn
50g (1¾oz) – 140m (153yds) of 100% cotton yarn in brown
50g (1¾oz) – 140m (153yds) of 100% cotton yarn in dark-brown
50g (1¾oz) – 140m (153yds) of 100% cotton yarn in red
1.5mm (US 8) crochet hook
2mm (US 4) crochet hook
1 removable stitch marker
SIZE: 9.5cm (3¾in) diameter
TENSION: Work 3 sts and 2 rows of htr to measure 1cm (½in) square

INSTRUCTIONS

Start with a magic ring. Crochet in a continual spiral, without closing the previous round. Use a marker to indicate the start of each round, moving it as the work progresses.

PATCH

Rnds 1–6: work as for the circle for the Strawberry Patch, using brown cotton and a 2mm (US 4) hook.

Rnds 7–8: work as for the circle for the strawberry patch, using fawn cotton.

Rnds 9–10: work as for the circle for the strawberry patch, using off-white cotton.

Rnd 11: work as for the circle for the strawberry patch, using green cotton.

CHERRIES
(make 2)

Rnd 1: using red cotton and a 1mm hook, make a magic ring and ss to secure. 2 ch (counts as 1 htr), 7 htr in ring, ss to 2nd ch of t-ch to join. Pull yarn tail to close the ring

Rnd 2 (inc.): 1 ch, 2 dc in each st around (16 sts)

Fasten off and weave in ends.

STALKS

Using a 2mm (US 4) hook, join the brown cotton to any dc at the edge of a cherry. 1 ch, 1 dc, 12 ch, 2 htr in 3rd ch from hook, 3 htr, 6 ch, 1 dc in any dc of 2nd cherry.

Fasten off and weave in ends.

LEAF

Row 1: using green cotton and a 1.5mm (US 8) hook, join yarn with a ss to the first htr at start of left hand stalk. 3 ch (counts as 1 tr), 4 tr in base of ch, turn (5 sts)

Row 2: 2 ch, 2 htr in next st, 2htr, 2htr in the last st (7 sts)

Row 3: 2 ch, 4 htr, htr2tog (6 sts)

Row 4: 2 ch, 2 htr, htr3tog (4 sts)

Row 5: 2 ch, htr3tog

Fasten off and weave in ends.

Sew the stalks and cherries to the patch.

Leave the tip of the leaf detached from the circle to give a three-dimensional effect.

Flower Patch

YOU WILL NEED

50g (1¾oz) — 140m (153yds) of 100% cotton yarn in white
50g (1¾oz) — 140m (153yds) of 100% cotton yarn in brown
50g (1¾oz) — 140m (153yds) of 100% cotton yarn in black
50g (1¾oz) — 140m (153yds) of 100% cotton yarn in green
50g (1¾oz) — 140m (153yds) of 100% cotton yarn in red
0.8mm (US 14) crochet hook
1.5mm (US 8) crochet hook
SIZE: 5cm (2in) diameter
TENSION: Work 6 sts and 5 rows of htr to measure 1cm (½in) square

INSTRUCTIONS

Start with a magic ring. Crochet in a continual spiral, without closing the previous round. Use a marker to indicate the start of each round, moving it as the work progresses.

PATCH

Rnds 1 to 6: work as for the circle for the strawberry patch, using brown cotton
Rnds 7–8: work as for the circle for the strawberry patch, using white cotton
Rnds 9–10: work as for the circle for the strawberry patch, using black cotton
Rnd 11: work as for the circle for the strawberry patch, using white cotton

FLOWER

Using red cotton and a 0.8mm (US 14) crochet hook, 3 ch
Row 1: 3 htr in 3rd ch from hook, turn (4 sts)
Row 2: 2 ch, 2 htr in next st, 1 htr, 2 htr in the last st, turn (6 sts)
Row 3: 2 ch, 2 htr in next st, 2 htr, 2 htr in next st, 1 htr in last st, turn (8 sts)
Row 4: 2 ch, htr across, turn (8 sts)
Row 5: 2 ch, htr2tog, 3 htr, htr2tog, turn (6 sts)
Row 6: 2 ch, htr2tog, 1 htr, htr2tog (4 sts)
Fasten off and weave in ends.

STALK

Using green yarn and a 1.5mm (US 8) hook, 7 ch, ss in 3rd ch from hook.

LEAVES

6 ch, 2 trtr in 2 ch-sp at top of stalk, 6 ch, ss in 2 ch-sp, repeat from * to * twice more. Fasten off, leaving a long tail. Use tail to attach stalk and leaves to flower.

Sew stalk and flower to centre of patch.

Tiny Star

YOU WILL NEED
50g (1¾oz) – 140m (153yds) of 100% cotton yarn in off-white
1.25mm crochet hook (please note that there is no US crochet hook size equivalent for this size. The closest is a US 10)
1 removable stitch marker
SIZE: 4.5cm (1¾in) diameter
TENSION: WORK 4 sts and 4 rows of dc to measure 1cm (½in) square

INSTRUCTIONS

Start with a magic ring. Crochet in a continual spiral, without closing the previous round. Use a marker to indicate the start of each round, moving it as the work progresses.

CENTRE

Rnd 1: using off-white cotton and a 1.25mm crochet hook, make a magic ring and ss to secure. 1 ch, 8 dc in ring, pull yarn tail to close the ring (8 sts)

Rnd 2: 2 dc in each st around (16 sts)

Rnd 3: *2 dc in next dc, 3dc*, rep from * to * three more times, ss in first dc to join (20 sts)

POINTS

Row 1: 1 ch, 4 dc, turn.

Row 2: 1 ch, miss one st, 3 dc, turn

Row 3: 1 ch, miss one st, 2 dc, turn

Row 4: 1 ch, miss one st, 1 dc

Fasten off and weave in ends.

Make the next point by rejoining yarn in next edge stitch after the point just worked. Repeat Rows 1–4 four more times (5 points made). Do not fasten off after the last point worked, but continue as follows:

FINISHING OFF

1 ch, dc evenly around the points of the star.

Fasten off and weave in ends.

Small Star

YOU WILL NEED
50g (1¾oz) – 140m (153yds) of 100% cotton yarn in yellow
1.5mm (US 8) crochet hook
1 removable stitch marker
SIZE: 5cm (2in) diameter
TENSION: Work 3 sts and 3 rows of dc to measure 1cm (½in) square

INSTRUCTIONS

Start with a magic ring. Crochet in a continual spiral, without closing the previous round. Use a marker to indicate the start of each round, moving it as the work progresses.

CENTRE

Rnd 1: using yellow cotton and a 1.5mm (US 8) hook, make a magic ring and ss to secure. 1 ch, 10 dc in ring, pull on yarn tail to close the ring (10 sts)

Rnd 2: 2 dc in each st around (20 sts)

Rnd 4: *2 dc in next st, 3 dc*, repeat from * to * four more times, ss in first dc to join (25 sts)

POINTS

Row 1: 1 ch, 5 dc, turn

Row 2: 1 ch, miss one st, 4 dc, turn

Row 3: 1 ch, miss one st, 3 dc, turn

Row 4: 1 ch, miss one st, 2 dc, turn

Row 5: 1 ch, miss one st, 1 dc

Fasten off and weave in ends.

Make next point by rejoining yarn in next edge stitch after the point just worked. Repeat Rows 1–5 four more times (5 points made). Do not fasten off after the last point worked, but continue as follows:

FINISHING OFF

1 ch, dc evenly around the points of the star.

Fasten off and weave in ends.

Medium Star

YOU WILL NEED

50g (1¾oz) — 140m (153yds) of 100% cotton yarn in red
1.25mm crochet hook (please note that there is no US crochet hook size equivalent for this size. The closest is a US 10)
1.5mm (US 8) crochet hook
1 removable stitch marker
SIZE: 6cm (2½in) diameter
TENSION: Work 4 sts and 4 rows of dc to measure 1cm (½in) square

INSTRUCTIONS

Start with a magic ring. Crochet in a continual spiral, without closing the previous round. Use a marker to indicate the start of each round, moving it as the work progresses.

CENTRE

Rnd 1: using red cotton and a 1.25mm hook, make a magic ring and ss to secure. 1 ch, 14 dc in ring, pull on yarn tail to close the ring (14 sts)
Rnd 2: 2 dc in each st around (28 sts)
Rnd 3: dc around (28 sts)
Rnd 4: *2 dc in next st, 13 dc*, repeat from * to *, ss to first dc to join (30 sts)

POINTS

Row 1: 6 dc, turn
Row 2: 1 ch, miss one st, 5 dc, turn
Row 3: 1 ch, miss one st, 4 dc, turn
Row 4: 1 ch, miss one st, 3 dc, turn
Row 5: 1 ch, miss one st, 2 dc, turn
Row 6: 1 ch, miss one st, 1 dc, turn
Fasten off and weave in ends.
Make the next point by rejoining yarn in next edge stitch after the point just worked. Repeat Rows 1–6 four more times (5 points made). Do not fasten off after the last point worked, but continue as follows:

FINISHING OFF

1 ch, dc evenly around the points of the star.
Fasten off and weave in ends.

Large Star

YOU WILL NEED
50g (1¾oz) – 140m (153yds) of 100% cotton yarn in purple
1.25mm (US 10) crochet hook
1.5mm (US 8) crochet hook
1 removable stitch marker
SIZE: 7.5cm (3in) diameter
TENSION: Work 3 sts and 3 rows of dc to measure 1cm (½in) square

INSTRUCTIONS

Start with a magic ring. Crochet in a continual spiral, without closing the previous round. Use a marker to indicate the start of each round, moving it as the work progresses.

CENTRE
Rnd 1: using red cotton and a 1.25mm (US 10) hook, make a magic ring and ss to secure. 1 ch, 14 dc in ring, pull yarn tail to close the ring (14 sts)

Rnd 2: 2 dc in each st around (28 sts)

Rnd 3: dc around (28 sts)

Rnd 4: *2 dc in next st, 3 dc*, rep from * to * around (35 sts)

Rnd 5: dc around, ss to first dc to join

POINTS
Row 1: 7 dc, turn

Row 2: 1 ch, miss one st, 6 dc, turn

Row 3: 1 ch, miss one st, 5 dc, turn

Row 4: 1 ch, miss one st, 4 dc, turn

Row 5: 1 ch, miss one st, 3 dc, turn

Row 6: 1 ch, miss one st, 2 dc, turn

Row 7: 1 ch, miss one st, 1 dc, turn

Fasten off and weave in yarn.

Make next point by rejoining yarn in next edge stitch after the point just worked. Repeat Rows 1–7 four more times (5 points made). Do not fasten off, but continue as follows:

FINISHING OFF
1 ch, dc evenly around the points of the star.

Fasten off and weave in ends.

Skull

YOU WILL NEED
50g (1¾oz) – 140m (153yds) of 100% cotton yarn in yellow
1 skein each of red and black Mouliné DMC embroidery floss
1.5mm (US 8) crochet hook
1 removable stitch marker
1 button (approximately 1cm/½in in diameter)
Tapestry needle
SIZE: 3.5 x 4.5cm (1½ x 1¾in)
TENSION: Work 4 sts and 3 rows of htr to measure 1cm (½in) square

INSTRUCTIONS

Start with a magic ring. Crochet in a continual spiral, without closing the previous round. Use a marker to indicate the start of each round, moving it as the work progresses.

Rnd 1: make a magic ring, ss to secure. 2 ch (counts as 1 htr), 11 htr in ring, pull on yarn tail to close the ring (12 sts)

Rnd 2: 2 htr in each st around (24 sts)

Rnd 3: htr around (24 sts)

Rnd 4 (inc.): 4 htr, 2 htr in next st, 1 htr, 2 htr in next st, 17 htr (26 sts)

Rnd 5: 2 htr, 2 htr in next st, 6 htr, 2 htr in next st, 14 htr, 2 htr in next st, 1 htr, ss to first htr to join (29 sts)

Make bottom section, working back and forth in rows.

Row 1: 2 ch, 1 htr in base of ch, 4 htr, 2 htr in next st, turn (8 sts)

Rows 2–3: 2 ch, 7 htr, turn

Fasten off and weave in ends.

EMBROIDERY

Embroider a long cross stitch, using three strands of red embroidery floss for one of the eyes.

For the second eye, sew on the button using white thread.

For the mouth, embroider one long straight stitch using three strands of black floss, slashed with three short straight stitches.

Lightning Bolt

YOU WILL NEED
50g (1¾oz) — 140m (153yds) of 100% cotton yarn in yellow
0.8mm (US 14) crochet hook
SIZE: 6 x 2cm (2½ x ¾in)
TENSION: Work 5 sts and 1 row of tr to measure 1cm (½in) wide by 0.5cm (¼in) high

INSTRUCTIONS

Row 1: 37 ch, 1 htr in 3rd ch from hook, 2 htr, 5 tr in next ch, 11 tr, tr5tog, 4 tr, 5 tr in next ch, 1 tr, 2 tr in next ch, 1 tr, 2 htr in next ch, 2 htr, 2 dc, ss in last ch, turn

Row 2: ss in first 2 dc's in previous row, 7 dc, 2 htr, 3 htr in next st, 2 htr in next st, 6 htr, miss group of tr5tog and 1 tr in previous row, 1 ss in next tr, 1 dc, 3 dc in next st, 5 dc

FINISHING OFF

1 ch, dc evenly around the edges, ss to first dc to join. Fasten off and weave in ends.

Bow

YOU WILL NEED
50g (1¾oz) — 140m (153yds) of 100% cotton yarn in pink
1.5mm (US 8) crochet hook
Tapestry needle
SIZE: 5 x 2cm (2 x ¾in)
TENSION: Work 3 sts and 3 rows of dc to measure 1cm (½in) square

INSTRUCTIONS

Work back and forth in rows.

Row 1: 17 ch, 1 dc in 2nd ch from hook and in each ch across (16 sts)

Rows 2–7: 1 ch, dc across (16 sts)

Fasten off and weave in ends.

FINISHING OFF

Thread needle with a double piece of pink sewing thread and attach to the edge of crocheted rectangle, halfway along one of its long sides. Wrap this thread around the rectangle so as to give it a bow shape and fasten off the thread on the wrong side of the work.

TIP

A bow is one of the simplest and quickest motifs to make, so it's ideal for beginners. Practise and make several of them, so you learn how to crochet regular, even stitches. Why not link them together to make a pretty garland to show off your new skills?

Sun

YOU WILL NEED

50g (1¾oz) – 140m (153yds) of 100% cotton yarn in yellow

1 skein of black cotton embroidery floss

1.5mm (US 8) crochet hook

1 removable stitch marker

Tapestry needle

SIZE: 6.5cm (2½in) diameter

TENSION: Work 4 sts and 2 rows of htr to measure 1cm (½in) square

INSTRUCTIONS

Start with a magic ring. Crochet in a continual spiral, without closing the previous round. Use a marker to indicate the start of each round, moving it as the work progresses.

Rnd 1: make a magic ring, ss to secure. 2 ch, 10 htr in ring, pull on yarn tail to close the ring (11 sts)

Rnd 2: 2 htr in each st around (22 sts)

Rnd 3: htr around (22 sts)

Rnd 4: *2 htr in next st, 1 htr*, rep from * to * to last 2 sts, 2 htr in next 2 sts (34 sts)

Rnd 5: *1 dc, 14 ch, miss next st*, repeat from * to * around, ss in first dc to join

Fasten off and weave in ends.

EMBROIDERY

Embroider the eyes and mouth using two strands of black embroidery floss by doing several short straight stitches.

Candy

YOU WILL NEED
50g (1¾oz) – 140m (153yds) of 100% cotton yarn in off-white
50g (1¾oz) – 140m (153yds) of 100% cotton yarn in pink
1.5mm (US 8) crochet hook
1 removable stitch marker
SIZE: 6.5 x 3.5cm (2½ x 1½in)
TENSION: Work 3 sts and 3 rows of htr to measure 1cm (½in) square

INSTRUCTIONS

Start with a magic ring. Use a marker to indicate the start of each round, moving it as the work progresses.

CENTRE

Rnd 1: using off-white cotton, make a magic ring and ss to secure. 2 ch, 8 htr in ring, ss in 2nd ch of t-ch to join. Pull on yarn tail to close the ring. Fasten off (9 sts)

Rnd 2: join dark pink cotton to any st, 2 ch, htr in base of ch, *2 htr in each st around, ss to 2nd ch of t-ch to join. Fasten off yarn (18 sts)

Rnd 3: join off-white cotton, 2 ch, htr around, ss to 2nd ch of t-ch to join.
Fasten off and weave in ends.

SIDE PIECES

Row 1: rejoin dark pink yarn to last st on Rnd 3, 2 ch, 5 htr in base of ch, turn (6 sts)

Row 2: 3 ch, 1tr in base of ch, 1 tr, *2 tr in next st, 1 tr*, rep from * to *, turn (9 sts)

Row 3: 3 ch, 2 tr in each of next 7 sts, 1 tr in last st
Fasten off and weave in ends.

Rejoin dark pink yarn on opposite side of the candy and repeat Rows 1–3.

Smiley Face

YOU WILL NEED
50g (1¾oz) – 140m (153yds) of 100% cotton yarn in orange
1 skein of black Mouliné DMC embroidery floss
1.25mm crochet hook (please note that there is no US crochet hook size equivalent for this size. The closest is a US 10)
1 removable stitch marker
Tapestry needle
SIZE: 3.5cm (1½in) diameter
TENSION: Work 4 sts and 3 rows of htr to measure 1cm (½in) square

INSTRUCTIONS

Start with a magic ring. Crochet in a continual spiral, without closing the previous round. Use a marker to indicate the start of each round, moving it as the work progresses.

Rnd 1: make a magic ring and ss to secure. 2 ch, 9 htr in ring, pull yarn tail to close the ring (10 sts)

Rnd 2: 2 dc in each st around (20 sts)

Rnd 3: dc around (20 sts)

Rnd 4: *1 dc, 2 dc in next st*, repeat from * to * around (30 sts)

Rnd 5: dc around, ss in first dc to join
Fasten off and weave in ends.

EMBROIDERY

For the eyes, do several short straight stitches, all the same length, using two strands of black floss.

For the mouth, embroider little stem stitches, following the outline of half of Rnd 1, using two strands of black floss.

Infinity Loop

YOU WILL NEED
50g (1¾oz) – 140m (153yds) of 100% cotton yarn in orange
1mm (US 12) crochet hook
Tapestry needle
SIZE: 6 x 2cm (2½ x ¾in)

INSTRUCTIONS

Row 1: 51 ch, 1 dc in 2nd ch from hook and in each ch across (50 sts)
Fasten off, leaving a 15cm (6in) tail.

FINISHING OFF
Lay the strip of crochet flat then sew the ends together to form a ring. Twist the circle so that the stitching is in the middle of the figure of '8' and sew a few stitches to hold it in shape.

Flowers

YOU WILL NEED

50g (1¾oz) – 140m (153yds) of 100% cotton yarn in yellow
50g (1¾oz) – 140m (153yds) of 100% cotton yarn in pink
50g (1¾oz) – 140m (153yds) of 100% cotton yarn in orange
1.5mm (US 8) crochet hook
1 removable stitch marker
SIZE: various
TENSION: Work 4 sts and 1 row of htr to measure 1cm (½in) square

INSTRUCTIONS FOR SMALL FLOWER

Rnd 1: using yellow cotton, make a magic ring and ss to secure. 3 ch (counts as 1 tr), 11 tr in ring, ss in 3rd ch of t-ch, pull on yarn tail to close the ring (12 sts)

Rnd 2: 1 ch, *1 dc, 2 ch, miss next st*, repeat from * to * five more times, ss in first dc to join (six 2 ch-sps)

Rnd 3: *ss in next 2 ch-sp, 1 ch, 1 dc, 1 htr, 5 tr, 1 htr*, repeat from * to * five more times, ss in first dc to join

Fasten off and weave in ends.

INSTRUCTIONS FOR MEDIUM FLOWER

Rnds 1–3: using orange cotton, work as for the small yellow flower

Rnd 4: (work using Row 2 as base), *ss into next 2 ch-sp, 1 ch, 1 dc, 3 ch, skip petal in rnd 3*, repeat from * to * four times, 3 ch, miss 4 sts of petal in Rnd 3, 1 dc between sts, 3 ch, miss last 3 sts of petal, ss in first dc to join (seven 3 ch-sps)

Rnd 5: *ss in next 3 ch-sp, 1 ch, 1 dc, 1 htr, 7 tr, 1 htr*, rep from * to * six more times, ss in first dc to join

Fasten off and weave in ends.

INSTRUCTIONS FOR LARGE FLOWER

Start with a magic ring. Crochet in a continual spiral, without closing the previous round. Use a marker to indicate the start of each round, moving it as the work progresses.

Rnds 1–3: using pink cotton, work as for the small yellow flower

Rnds 4–5: work as for the medium orange flower

Rnd 6: (work using Row 4 as base), *ss in next 3 ch-sp, 1 ch, 1 dc, 3 ch, miss petal in Rnd 5*, rep from * to * five times, 3 ch, miss 4 sts of petal in Rnd 5, 1 dc between sts, 4 ch, miss last sts of petal, ss in first dc to join (eight 4ch-sps)

Rnd 7: *ss in next 4 ch-sp, 1 ch, 1 dc, 1 htr, 7 tr, 1 htr*, repeat from * to * seven more times, ss in first dc to join

Fasten off and weave in ends.

TIP

For an eye-catching and unique accessory, make about fifteen flowers of different sizes and colours. Take a scarf and position them at both ends, packing them close together so you can hardly see the scarf below any more. Stitch them in place carefully, using blind stitching. It's an easy way to warm and brighten up a cold, winter day!

Owl

YOU WILL NEED
50g (1¾oz) – 140m (153yds) of 100% cotton yarn in yellow
50g (1¾oz) – 140m (153yds) of 100% cotton yarn in orange
50g (1¾oz) – 140m (153yds) of 100% cotton yarn in brown
50g (1¾oz) – 140m (153yds) of 100% cotton yarn in green
50g (1¾oz) – 140m (153yds) of 100% cotton yarn in off-white
50g (1¾oz) – 140m (153yds) of 100% cotton yarn in purple
1mm (US 12) crochet hook
1.5mm (US 8) crochet hook
SIZE: 6 x 3.5cm (2½ x 3½in)
TENSION: Work 4 sts and 4 rows of htr to measure 1cm (½in) square

INSTRUCTIONS

Work the first row on each side of the foundation chain, then work back and forth in rows.

BODY

Row 1: using yellow cotton and a 1.5mm (US 8) crochet hook, 16 ch, 1 htr in 3rd ch from hook, 12 htr, 4 htr in last ch, turn and work on the underside of the chain as follows: 12 htr, 2 htr in last ch. Fasten off (33 sts)

Row 2: join the orange cotton to the last st of row 1, 2 ch, 1 htr in base of ch, 12 htr, *2 htr in next st, 1 htr*, repeat from * to * two more times, 12 htr, 2 htr in last st, turn (38 sts)

Row 3: 2 ch, 1 htr in base of ch, 16 htr, 2 htr in next st, 2 htr, 2 htr in next st, 16 htr, 2 htr in last st. Fasten off (42 sts)

Row 4: join brown cotton to last st of row 3, 2 ch, 1htr in base of ch, 18 htr, 2 htr in next st, 2 htr, 2 htr in next st, 18 htr, 2 htr in last st, turn (46 sts)

Row 5: 2 ch, 1 htr in base of ch, 44 htr, 2 htr in last st . Fasten off (48 sts)

Row 6: join green cotton to last st of row 5, 2 ch, 1 htr in base of ch, 17 htr, *2 htr in next st, 1 htr*, repeat from * to * four times, 2 htr in next st, 18 htr, 2 htr in last st, turn (56 sts)

Fasten off and weave in ends

Row 7: 2 ch, 1 htr in base of ch, 1 htr in each st across, 2 htr in last st (55 sts)

Edging: Using green yarn, 1 ch, dc evenly around the edge. Fasten off and weave in ends.

EYES

(make 2)

Rnd 1: using brown cotton and a 1mm (US 12) crochet hook, make a magic ring and ss to secure. 2 ch, 7 htr in ring, ss in 2nd ch of t-ch to join (8 sts)

Fasten off and weave in ends.

Rnd 2: join off-white cotton to any st in Rnd 1, 2 ch, 1 htr in base of ch, 2 htr in each st around, ss to 2nd ch of t-ch to join (16 sts)

Fasten off and weave in ends.

Rnd 3: join purple cotton to any st in Rnd 2, 2 ch, 1 htr in each st around, ss in 2nd ch of t-ch to join (16 sts)

Fasten off, leaving a long tail.

Sew the eyes to body using tail, weave in ends.

FEET

Using a 1mm (US 12) hook and brown cotton, attach the yarn to the bottom of the body in a desired place (or 3 sts to the right of the centre st) and work as follows:

1 ch, *1 dc, 9 ch*, repeat from * to * twice more in the same st, ss in last dc to join.

Repeat to the left of centre st.

Fasten off and weave in ends.

Little Owl

YOU WILL NEED

50g (1¾oz) — 140m (153yds) of 100% cotton yarn in orange
50g (1¾oz) — 140m (153yds) of 100% cotton yarn in purple
1 ball each of orange and purple 100% cotton — 50g (1¾oz) — 140 m/153 yds
1 skein each of yellow and white Mouliné DMC cotton embroidery floss
1.5mm (US 8) crochet hook
1 removable stitch marker
Tapestry needle
SIZE: 6 x 5cm (2½ x 2in)
TENSION: to measure 1cm (½in) square 4 sts and 3 rows of htr

INSTRUCTIONS

Start with a magic ring. Crochet in a continual spiral, without closing the previous round. Use a marker to indicate the start of each round, moving it as the work progresses.

BODY

Rnd 1: using purple cotton and a 1.5mm (US 8) crochet hook, make a magic ring and ss to secure. 2 ch, 11 htr in ring, pull on yarn tail to close the ring (12 sts)

Rnd 2: 2 htr in each st around (24 sts)

Rnd 3: *2 htr in next st, 1 htr*, rep from * to * around (36 sts)

Rnd 4 (inc): *2 htr in next st, 2 htr*, around (48 sts)

Rnd 5: 1 htr in each st around (48 htr)

Rnd 6: *2 htr in next st, 3 htr*, rep from * to * around (60 sts)

Fasten off and weave in ends.

WINGS

Count 5 sts from last ss on previous rnd and **join purple cotton with a ss, 1 ch, 1 dc, 1 htr, *2 tr in next st, 1 tr*, repeat from * to * 3 times, 2 tr in next st.**, fasten off.

Count 12 sts from the wing that you have just made, repeat from ** to **.

Fasten off and weave in ends.

EARS

Using orange cotton and a 1.5mm (US 8) crochet hook, miss 5 sts from top of wing and join yarn.

1 htr, 2 tr in next st, *2 dtr in next st*, rep from * to *, 2 tr in next st, 1 htr, fasten off. Count 6 sts from the ear that you have just made, rejoin yarn, repeat from ** to **.

Fasten off and weave in ends.

EMBROIDERY

For the eyes, sew three straight stitches, close together, using two strands of purple cotton for the pupils and (using two strands of white embroidery floss) work 0.5cm (¼in) straight stitches for the whites.

For the beak, using two strands of yellow embroidery floss, embroider four straight stitches, all starting at the centre stitch.

TIP

Get inspiration from The Gallery at the beginning of the book and have fun with colours.

If you use different weights of cotton yarn or crochet using a double strand, you can also very easily change the size of the motif or why not make a little pocket patch to sew on a garment?

Bear

YOU WILL NEED

50g (1¾oz) – 140m (153yds) of 100% cotton yarn in purple
50g (1¾oz) – 140m (153yds) of 100% cotton yarn in yellow
50g (1¾oz) – 140m (153yds) of 100% cotton yarn in orange
100% cotton – 50g (1¾oz) – 140 m/153 yds
1 skein each of black and white Mouliné DMC embroidery floss
1.25mm crochet hook (please note that there is no US crochet hook size equivalent for this size. The closest is a US 10)
1.5mm (US 8) crochet hook
1 removable stitch marker
Tapestry needle
SIZE: 5 x 5.5cm (2 x 2¼in)
TENSION: Work 4 sts and 4 rows of htr to measure 1cm (½in) square

INSTRUCTIONS

Start with a magic ring. Crochet in a continual spiral, without closing the previous round. Use a marker to indicate the start of each round, moving it as the work progresses.

HEAD

Rnd 1: using purple cotton and a 1.5mm (US 8) crochet hook, make a magic ring and ss to secure. 2 ch, 11 htr in ring, pull on yarn tail to close the ring (12 sts)

Rnd 2: 2 htr in each st around (24 sts)

Rnd 3: *2 htr in next st, 1 htr*, rep from * to * around (36 sts)

Rnd 4 (inc): *2 htr in next st, 2 htr*, around (48 sts)

Rnd 5: 1 htr in each st around (48 htr)

Rnd 6: *2 htr in next st, 3 htr*, rep from * to * around (60 sts)

Rnd 7: 1 htr in each st around, ss in first htr to join (60 sts)

Fasten off and weave in ends.

EARS

Using yellow cotton and a 1.5mm (US 8) crochet hook, join yarn to last st worked on Rnd 7.

1 htr, 2tr in next st, *2 dtr in next st*, rep from * to *, 2 tr in next st, 1 htr, fasten off. Count 7 sts from the ear that you have just made, rejoin yarn, repeat from ** to **.

Fasten off and weave in ends.

MUZZLE

Using orange cotton and a 1.25mm (US 10) crochet hook, work as follows:

Row 1: 3 ch, 6 htr in 3rd ch from hook, turn (7 sts)

Row 2: 2 ch, 2 htr in each of next 5 sts, 1 htr, turn (12 sts)

Row 3: 2 ch, 2 htr in next st, 8 htr, 2 htr in next st, 1 tr, turn (14 sts)

Row 4: 2 ch, 13 htr, turn (14 sts)

Row 5: 2 ch, 1 htr, *2 htr in next st, 1 htr*, repeat from * to * four more times, 2 htr (16 sts)

Row 6: 2 ch, 2 htr in next st, 12 htr. 2 htr in next st, 1 htr in last st (18 sts)

Fasten off and weave in ends.

EMBROIDERY

Use two strands of white floss to embroider the outline of the eyes with two oval shapes in stem stitch and create the pupils using straight stitch, sewn very close together.

Embroider a curved mouth on the muzzle in stem stitch, using two strands of black floss and then do a short, straight stitch to create a vertical line above it. Sew the muzzle onto the head.

TIP

These little motifs are perfect for customizing a child's scarf, hat or jumper. They could even be used to hide a stain or tear. To do this, match the colours for the motifs with the colour of the garment or item.

Snail

YOU WILL NEED
50g (1¾oz) – 140m (153yds) of 100% cotton yarn in green
1 skein of black cotton Mouliné DMC embroidery floss
1mm (US 12) crochet hook
1.25mm (US 10) crochet hook
1.5mm (US 8) crochet hook
1 removable stitch marker
Tapestry needle
SIZE: 6 x 5cm (2½ x 2in)
TENSION: Work 4 sts and 2 rows of htr to measure 1cm (½in) square

INSTRUCTIONS

Start with a magic ring. Crochet in a continual spiral, without closing the previous round. Use a marker to indicate the start of each round, moving it as the work progresses.

SHELL

Rnd 1: using green cotton and a 1.5mm (US 8) crochet hook, make a magic ring and ss to secure. 2 ch, 12 htr in ring, pull on yarn tail to close the ring (13 sts)

Rnd 2: 2 htr in each st around (26 sts)

Rnd 3: 2 htr in next st, 25 htr

HEAD

Continue by working back and forth in rows, using a 1.25mm (US 10) hook as follows:

Row 1: 1 htr in next st, 8 ch

Row 2: 1 htr in 3rd ch from hook, 6 htr, join this row to the circular piece with a ss in the last htr worked, turn

Row 3: 6 htr, turn

Row 4: 2 ch, 5 htr, ss to last ss of Row 2

Edging: 1 ch, dc evenly around, ss to first dc to join

Fasten off and weave in ends.

TAIL

With RS facing, rejoin green yarn to rear of snail with a ss, and 5 ch, turn, 1 dc in 3rd ch from hook, 2 dc, 1 htr in the edging dc, 17 dc, ss in next st. Fasten off and weave in ends.

EMBROIDERY

Embroider the eye using small straight stitches and two strands of black embroidery floss.

Make the snail's antenna using two strands of black embroidery floss and a 1mm (US 12) crochet hook. Join the yarn to the top of the head with a ss, 5 ch, fasten off the yarn, make a knot and thread the yarn through the ch sts using a running stitch.

Cherry Cupcake

YOU WILL NEED

50g (1¾oz) — 140m (153yds) of 100% cotton yarn in pink
50g (1¾oz) — 140m (153yds) of 100% cotton yarn in off-white
50g (1¾oz) — 140m (153yds) of 100% cotton yarn in yellow
1 skein of orange cotton Mouliné DMC embroidery floss
1.5mm (US 8) crochet hook
SIZE: 5 x 6cm (2 x 2½in)
TENSION: Work 4 sts and 4 rows of dc to measure 1cm (½in) square

INSTRUCTIONS

BOTTOM

Using yellow cotton and a 1.5mm (US 8) crochet hook, 10 ch.

Row 1: 2 dc in 2nd ch from hook, 7 dc, 2 dc in the last st, turn (11 sts)

Row 2: 1 ch, 10 dc, 2 dc in last st, turn (12 sts)

Row 3: 1 ch, 11 dc, 2 dc in last st, turn (13 sts)

Row 4: 1 ch, 12 dc, 2 dc in last st, turn. (14 sts)

Row 5: 1 ch, 13 dc, 2 dc in last st, turn (15 sts)

Row 6: 1 ch, 14 dc, 2 dc in last st, turn (16 sts)

Row 7: 1 ch, 15 dc, 2 dc in last st, turn (17 sts)

Row 8: 1 ch, dc across (17 sts)

Edging: 1 ch, and working down the side, along the bottom and up the other side, dc evenly across.

Fasten off and weave in ends.

TOP

Row 1: join off-white cotton to the first st worked in Row 8 with a ss. 3 ch, 4 tr in same st as base of ch, miss 3 sts, ss in next st, *3 ch, 4 tr in same st as base of ch, miss 2 sts, ss in next st*, rep from * to * three more times.

Fasten off and weave in ends.

Change to pink and work on the right side of previous row.

Row 2: with RS facing, join pink cotton to 3rd ch of first t-ch with a ss, 1 ch, 1 dc in same st, 3 tr in ss of Row 1, 1 dc in next tr, *3 tr in ss of Row 1, 1 dc in next tr*, rep from * to * two more times, 1 dc in next tr, turn

Continue working back and forth in rows as follows:

Row 3: 1 ch, *3 dc, miss 1 dc*, repeat from * to * three more times, turn (12 sts)

Row 4: 1 ch, miss next st, 10 dc

Row 5: 1 ch, miss next st, 9 dc, ss in next st

Fasten off and weave in ends.

CHERRY

Using orange cotton and a 1.5mm crochet hook, join yarn with a ss to the 5th dc on the Row 5, 3 ch, (2 tr, 2 dtr, 2 tr) in base of ch, 3 ch, ss to base of ch

Fasten off and weave in ends.

Flower Cupcake

YOU WILL NEED

50g (1¾oz) – 140m (153yds) of 100% cotton yarn in off-white
50g (1¾oz) – 140m (153yds) of 100% cotton yarn in pink
50g (1¾oz) – 140m (153yds) of 100% cotton yarn in blue
50g (1¾oz) – 140m (153yds) of 100% cotton yarn in orange
1mm (US 12) crochet hook
SIZE: 5 x 6cm (2 x 2½in)
TENSION: Work 4 sts and 4 rows of dc to measure 1cm (½in) square

INSTRUCTIONS

BOTTOM

Using orange cotton and a 1mm (US 12) crochet hook, 10 ch.

Rows 1 to 8: work as for the Cherry Cupcake, alternating between orange and blue every two rows. Fasten off and weave in ends each time

Row 9: rep Row 8

Edging: 1 ch and working down the side, along the bottom and up the other side, dc evenly across.

Fasten off and weave in ends.

TOP

Row 1: join pink cotton, 1 ch, 2 dc in first st, miss 1 st, 3 tr in next st, *miss 1 st, 1 dc in next st, 3 tr in next st*, repeat from * to * three times, miss 1 st, 2 dc in last st, turn

Row 2: 1 ch, miss 1 dc, 3 dc, *miss 1 tr, 3 tr in next dc, miss 1 tr, 1 dc in next tr*, repeat from * to * 3 times, miss 1 tr, 2 dc, turn. (17 sts)

Row 3: 1ch, miss 1 st, 2 dc, miss 1 tr, *1 dc in next tr, miss 1 tr, 3 tr in next dc, miss 1 tr*, rep from * to *, miss 1 tr, 3 dc, turn

Row 4: miss first dc, ss in next 2 dc, miss 1 tr, * 1 dc in next tr, miss 1 tr, 3tr in next dc, miss 1 tr*, rep from * to *, 1 dc in next dc, turn

Row 5: 1 ch, miss first dc and first tr, 1 dc in next tr, *miss 1 tr, 3 tr in next dc, miss 1 tr, 1 dc in next tr*, rep from * to *, ss in next tr, turn

Fasten off.

Rejoin pink cotton to the bottom of the 'frosting', 1 ch, dc around top of cupcake.

Fasten off and weave in ends.

LITTLE FLOWER

Using blue cotton, make a magic ring and ss to secure. 1 ch, *1 dc, 1 ch*, rep from * to * four more times, ss in first dc to join, pull on yarn tail to close the ring.

Petals: Join off-white cotton to any ch-sp, *1 dc, 3 ch, 2 tr, 3 ch, 1 dc, ss to next ch-sp*, rep from * to * four more times.

Fasten off and weave in ends.

Postion the flower as you onto the cupcake and sew in place.

Star Cupcake

YOU WILL NEED
50g (1¾oz) – 140m (153yds) of 100% cotton yarn in off-white
50g (1¾oz) – 140m (153yds) of 100% cotton yarn in blue
1 skein of orange cotton Mouliné DMC embroidery floss
1mm (US 12) crochet hook
1.5mm (US 8) crochet hook
Tapestry needle
SIZE: 5 x 6cm (2 x 2½in)
TENSION: Work 4 sts and 4 rows of dc to measure 1cm (½in) square

INSTRUCTIONS

BOTTOM

Using blue cotton and a 1.5mm (US 8) crochet hook, 10 ch

Rows 1 to 8: work as for the Cherry Cupcake, alternating between orange and blue every two rows. Fasten off and weave in ends each time

Row 9: 1 ch, 16 dc, 2 dc in last st (18 sts)

Row 10: 1 ch, 17 dc, 2 dc in last st (19 sts)

Edging: 1 ch, and working down the side, along the bottom and up the other side, dc evenly across.

Fasten off and weave in ends.

TOP

Row 1: using a 1.5mm (US 8) hook, join off-white cotton to last st worked of Row 10 above. 1 ch, 2 dc, *miss 1 st, 3 tr in next st, miss 1 st, 1 dc in next st*, rep from * to * three more times, 2 dc.

Fasten off and weave in ends.

Row 2: with RS facing, join blue cotton to first dc, 1 ch, 1 dc in each st across, turn (18 sts)

Row 3: 1 ch, miss 1 dc, 16 dc, turn

Row 4: 1 ch, miss 1 dc, 14 dc, turn

Row 5: 1 ch, miss 1 dc, 12 dc, turn

Row 6: 1 ch, miss 1 dc, 10 dc, turn

Row 7: 1 ch, miss 1 dc, 8 dc, turn

Row 8: 1 ch, miss 1 dc, 6 dc, turn

Row 9: 1 ch, miss 1 dc, 4 dc

Fasten off and weave in ends.

Using blue cotton, rejoin the yarn to first tr on Row 1, 1 ch, 1 dc, *3 tr in base of dc at end of next row, miss this row, 1 dc in first st of next row*, repeat from * to * three more times, doing last dc in first st of Row 9, 2 tr in next st three times, 1 dc in last st of this same row. Continue working on other side: 3 tr in base of first dc on Row 9, *1 dc in dc at end of next row, 3tr in base of dc at end of next row*, rep from * to * twice more, finish with 1 dc in last tr on Row 2.

Fasten off and weave in ends.

LITTLE STAR

Using orange embroidery floss and a 1mm (US 12) crochet hook, make a magic ring and ss to secure. 2 ch, 9 htr in ring, ss in 2nd ch of t-ch to join, pull on yarn tail to close the ring (10 sts).

Points of star: *6 ch, ss in 2nd ch from hook, 1 dc, 2 htr, 1 tr, miss 1 dc on rnd, ss in next st*, repeat from * to * four more times.

Fasten off and weave in ends. Sew the star to the top of the cupcake.

EMBROIDERY

Embroider each star, sewing five short straight stitches in the shape of a star, using three strands of orange embroidery floss.

Tiny Bird

YOU WILL NEED

50g (1¾oz) – 140m (153yds) of 100% cotton yarn in orange
50g (1¾oz) – 140m (153yds) of 100% cotton yarn in purple
1 skein of black Mouliné DMC embroidery floss
1mm (US 12) crochet hook
1.5mm (US 8) crochet hook
1 removable stitch marker
Tapestry needle
SIZE: 3.5 x 2cm (1½ x ¾in)
TENSION: Work 3 sts and 3 rows of htr to measure 1cm (½in) square

INSTRUCTIONS

Start with a magic ring. Crochet in a continual spiral, without closing the previous round. Use a marker to indicate the start of each round, moving it as the work progresses.

BODY

Rnd 1: using orange cotton and a 1.5mm (US 8) hook, make a magic ring and ss to secure. 2 ch, 7 htr in ring, pull on yarn tail to close the ring (8 sts)

Rnd 2: 2 dc in each st around (16 sts)

Rnd 3: 2 dc in next dc, 3 dc

TAIL

Continue working in orange cotton and crochet back and forth in rows.

Row 1: 1 ch, 3 dc, turn

Row 2: 1 ch, 2 dc, turn

Row 3: 1 ch, 1 dc

Edging: 1 ch, dc evenly around, ss in first dc to join.

Fasten off and weave in ends.

BEAK

Using purple yarn and a 1mm (US 12) crochet hook, miss 4 sts from base of tail and attach yarn with a ss.

Row 1: 1 ch, 2 dc in next st, 1 dc, 2 dc in next st (5 sts)

Row 2: 1 ch, miss 1 st, 3 dc (3 sts)

Row 3: 1 ch, miss 1 st, 1 dc

Fasten off and weave in ends.

Rejoin purple yarn to the base of the beak, 1 ch, dc evenly around the beak, ss to the body to join.

Fasten off and weave in ends.

EMBROIDERY

For the eye, embroider a little dot in satin stitch, using three strands of embroidery floss.

Small Bird

YOU WILL NEED

50g (1¾oz) – 140m (153yds) of 100% cotton yarn in orange
50g (1¾oz) – 140m (153yds) of 100% cotton yarn in purple
1 skein of black Mouliné DMC embroidery floss
1mm (US 12) crochet hook
1.5mm (US 8) crochet hook
1 removable stitch marker
Tapestry needle
SIZE: 5 x 3.5cm (2 x 1½in)
TENSION: Work 3 sts and 3 rows of htr to measure 1cm (½in) square

INSTRUCTIONS

Start with a magic ring. Crochet in a continual spiral, without closing the previous round. Use a marker to indicate the start of each round, moving it as the work progresses.

BODY

Rnd 1: using orange cotton and a 1.5mm (US 8) hook, make a magic ring and ss to secure. 2 ch, 7 htr in ring, pull on yarn tail to close the ring (8 sts)

Rnd 2: 2 dc in each st around (16 sts)

Rnd 3: *2 dc in next st, 1 dc*, rep from * to * around (24 sts)

Rnd 4: *2 dc in next st*, 5 dc, rep from * to *, 4 dc, rep from * to *, 3 dc

TAIL

Continue working in orange cotton and crochet back and forth in rows.

Row 1: 1 ch, 2 dc in next st, 4dc, turn

Row 2: 1 ch, miss 1 dc, 4 dc, turn

Row 3: 1 ch, miss 1 st, 3 dc, turn

Row 4: 1 ch, miss 1 st, 2 dc, turn

Row 5: 1 ch, miss 1 st, 1 dc

Edging: 1 ch, dc evenly around, ss in first dc to join.

Fasten off and weave in ends.

BEAK

Using purple yarn and a 1mm (US 12) crochet hook, miss 8 sts from the base of the tail and join yarn with a ss in next dc.

Row 1: 1 ch, 4 dc, turn

Row 2: 1 ch, miss 1 st, 3 dc, turn

Row 3: 1 ch, miss 1 st, 2 dc

Fasten off.

Rejoin purple yarn to the base of the beak, 1 ch, dc evenly around the beak, ss to the body to join. Fasten off and weave in ends.

EMBROIDERY

For the eye, embroider a little dot in satin stitch, using three strands of embroidery floss.

Medium Bird

YOU WILL NEED
50g (1¾oz) – 140m (153yds) of 100% cotton yarn in orange
50g (1¾oz) – 140m (153yds) of 100% cotton yarn in purple
1 skein of black Mouliné DMC embroidery floss
1mm (US 12) crochet hook
1.5mm (US 8) crochet hook
1 removable stitch marker
Tapestry needle
SIZE: 5.5 x 4cm (2¼ x 1½in)
TENSION: Work 3 sts and 3 rows of htr to measure 1cm (½in) square

INSTRUCTIONS

Start with a magic ring. Crochet in a continual spiral, without closing the previous round. Use a marker to indicate the start of each round, moving it as the work progresses.

BODY

Rnd 1: using orange cotton and a 1.5mm (US 8) crochet hook, make a magic ring and ss to secure. 2 ch, 9 htr in ring, pull on yarn tail to close the ring (10 sts)

Rnd 2: 2 dc in each st around. (20 sts)

Rnd 3: *2 dc in next st, 1 dc*, rep from * to * around (30 sts)

Rnd 4: (inc): *2 dc in next st, 1 dc*, rep from * to * 10 times, 6dc

TAIL

Continue working in orange cotton, working in rows as follows:

Row 1: 1 ch, miss 1 st, 5 dc, turn

Row 2: 1 ch, miss 1 st, 4 dc, turn

Row 3: 1 ch, miss 1 st, 3 dc, turn

Row 4: 1 ch, miss 1 st, 2 dc

Edging: 1 ch, dc evenly around, ss in first dc to join.

Fasten off and weave in ends.

BEAK

Using purple yarn and a 1mm (US 12) crochet hook, miss 11 sts from the base of the tail and join yarn with a ss in next dc.

Row 1: 1 ch, 3 dc, 2 dc in next st, turn

Row 2: 1 ch, miss 1 st, 4 dc, turn

Row 3: 1 ch, miss 1 st, 3 dc

Fasten off.

Rejoin purple yarn to the base of the beak, 1 ch, dc evenly around the beak, ss to the body to join. Fasten off and weave in ends.

EMBROIDERY

For the eye, embroider a little dot in satin stitch, using two strands of embroidery floss.

Large Bird

YOU WILL NEED
50g (1¾oz) — 140m (153yds) of 100% cotton yarn in orange
50g (1¾oz) — 140m (153yds) of 100% cotton yarn in purple
1 skein of black Mouliné DMC embroidery floss
1mm (US 12) crochet hook
1.5mm (US 8) crochet hook
1 removable stitch marker
Tapestry needle
SIZE: 7.5 x 5cm (3 x 2in)
TENSION: Work 3 sts and 3 rows of htr to measure 1cm (½in) square

INSTRUCTIONS

Start with a magic ring. Crochet in a continual spiral, without closing the previous round. Use a marker to indicate the start of each round, moving it as the work progresses.

BODY

Rnd 1: using orange cotton and a 1.5mm (US 8) crochet hook, make a magic ring and ss to secure. 2 ch, 11 htr in ring, pull on yarn tail to close the ring (12 sts)

Rnd 2: 2 dc in each st around (24 sts)

Rnd 3: *2 dc in next st, 1 dc*, rep from * to * around (36 sts)

Rnd 4: *2 dc in next st, 2 dc*, rep from * to * around (48 sts)

Rnd 5: 4 dc, *2 dc in next st, 5 dc*, rep from * to * four more times, 2 dc, 2 dc in next st, 6 dc

TAIL

Continue working in orange cotton and crochet back and forth in rows.

Row 1: 1 ch, miss 1 dc, 6 dc, turn

Row 2: 1 ch, miss 1 st, 5 dc, turn

Row 3: 1 ch, miss 1 st, 4 dc, turn

Row 4: 1 ch, miss 1 st, 3 dc, turn

Row 5: 1 ch, miss 1 st, 2 dc

Edging: 1 ch, dc evenly around, ss in first dc to join.

Fasten off and weave in ends.

BEAK

Using purple yarn and a 1mm (US 12) crochet hook, miss 15 sts from the base of the tail and join yarn with a ss in next dc.

Row 1: 1 ch, 5 dc, turn

Row 2: 1 ch, miss 1 st, 4 dc, turn

Row 3: 1 ch, miss 1 st, 3 dc, turn

Row 4: 1 ch, miss 1 st, 2 dc

Fasten off and weave in yarn.

Rejoin purple yarn to the base of the beak, 1 ch, dc evenly around the beak, ss to the body to join. Fasten off and weave in ends.

EMBROIDERY

For the eye, embroider a little dot in satin stitch, using two strands of embroidery floss.

Extra Large Bird

YOU WILL NEED

50g (1¾oz) – 140m (153yds) of 100% cotton yarn in blue
50g (1¾oz) – 140m (153yds) of 100% cotton yarn in yellow
1 skein of black Mouliné DMC embroidery floss
1.5mm (US 8) crochet hook
1 removable stitch marker
Tapestry needle
SIZE: 16 x 9.5cm (6¾ x 3¾in)
TENSION: Work 3 sts and 3 rows of htr to measure 1cm (½in) square

INSTRUCTIONS

Start with a magic ring. Crochet in a continual spiral, without closing the previous round. Use a marker to indicate the start of each round, moving it as the work progresses.

BODY

Rnd 1: using blue cotton and a 1.5mm (US 8) crochet hook, make a magic ring and ss to secure. 2 ch, 11 htr in ring, pull on yarn tail to close the ring (12 sts)

Rnd 2: 2 dc in each st around (24 sts)

Rnd 3: *2 dc in next st, 1 dc*, rep from * to * around (36 sts)

Rnd 4: dc around (36 sts)

Rnd 5: *2 dc in next st, 2 dc*, rep from * to * around (48 sts)

Rnd 6: dc around (48 sts)

Rnd 7: *2 dc in next st, 3 dc*, rep from * to * around (60 sts)

Rnd 8: dc around (60 sts)

Rnd 9: *2 dc in next st, 4 dc*, rep from * to * around (72 sts)

Rnd 10: dc around (72 sts)

Rnd 11: *2 dc in next st, 5 dc*, rep from * to * around (84 sts)

Rnd 12: dc around (84 sts)

Rnd 13: *2 dc in next st, 6 dc*, rep from * to * around (96 sts)

Rnd 14: dc around (96 sts)

Rnd 15: *2 dc in next st, 7 dc*, rep from * to * around (108 sts)

Rnd 16–17: dc around (108 sts)

TAIL

Work back and forth in rows as follows:

Row 1: 1 ch, 19 dc, turn

Row 2: 1 ch, miss 1 dc, 18 dc, turn

Row 3: 1 ch, miss 1 dc, 17 dc, turn

Row 4: 1 ch, miss 1 dc, 16 dc, turn

Row 5: 1 ch, miss 1 dc, 15 dc, turn

Row 6: 1 ch, miss 1 dc, 13 dc, turn

Row 7: 1 ch, miss 1 dc, 11 dc, turn

Row 8: 1 ch, miss 1 dc, 9 dc, turn

Row 9: 1 ch, miss 1 dc, 7 dc, turn

Row 10: 1 ch, miss 1 dc, 6 dc, turn

Row 11: 1 ch, miss 1 dc, 5 dc, turn

Row 12: 1 ch, miss 1 dc, 4 dc, turn

Row 13: 1 ch, miss 1 dc, 3 dc, turn

Row 14: 1 ch, miss 1 dc, 2 dc

Edging: 1 ch, dc evenly around, ss to first dc to join.

Fasten off and weave in ends.

BEAK

Using yellow yarn and a 1.5mm (US 8) crochet hook, miss 75 sts from the base of the tail and join yarn with a ss in next dc.

Row 1: 1 ch, 9 dc, turn.

Row 2: 1 ch, miss 1 st, 8 dc, turn

Row 3: 1 ch, miss 1 st, 7 dc, turn

Row 4: 1 ch, miss 1 st, 6 dc, turn

Row 5: 1 ch, miss 1 st, 5 dc, turn

Row 6: 1 ch, miss 1 st, 4 dc, turn

Row 7: 1 ch, miss 1 st, 3 dc, turn

Row 8: 1 ch, miss 1 st, 2 dc, turn

Fasten off and weave in ends.

Rejoin purple yarn to the base of the beak, 1 ch, dc evenly around the beak, ss to the body to join. Fasten off and weave in ends.

EMBROIDERY

For the eye, embroider a little dot in satin stitch, using three strands of embroidery floss.

Sheep

YOU WILL NEED

50g (1¾oz) – 140m (153yds) of 100% cotton yarn in brown
50g (1¾oz) – 140m (153yds) of 100% cotton yarn in off-white
50g (1¾oz) – 140m (153yds) of 100% cotton yarn in sky blue
1 skein of brown Mouliné DMC cotton embroidery floss
1.5mm (US 8) crochet hook
1 removable stitch marker
Tapestry needle
SIZE: 9.5cm x 16cm (3¾ x 6¼in)
TENSION: Work 3 sts and 2 rows of tr to measure 1cm (½in) square

INSTRUCTIONS

Start with a magic ring. Use a marker to indicate the start of each round, moving it as the work progresses.

BODY

Start with the little centre flower.

Rnd 1: using blue cotton, make a magic ring and ss to secure. 1 ch, 8 dc in ring, ss to first dc to join, pull on yarn tail to close the ring (8 sts)

Rnd 2 (inc): join brown cotton to any dc, 1 ch, 2 dc in each st around, ss in first dc to join (16 sts)

Rnd 3: *6 ch, dc2tog (by inserting hook for first dc into the 2nd ch from the hook), 3 htr, miss 1 st on Rnd 2, ss in next st*, rep from * to * seven more times. Fasten off and weave in ends (seven petals made)

Rnd 4: Join white yarn to any ss (working into Rnd 2, behind petals on Rnd 3), 1 ch, 1 dc *2 ch, miss 1 petal, 1dc in next ss on previous rnd*, repeat from * to * seven more times, ss in first dc to join. Fasten off and weave in ends

Rnd 5: ss in 2 ch-sp, 3 ch, 4 tr (attaching tip of flower with 1 ss, inserting hook behind the end st on petal before working 2nd tr), miss 1 dc, *5 tr in next 2 ch-sp, attaching petal in same way, miss 1 dc*, repeat from * to * six more times, ss in 3rd ch of t-ch to join. Fasten off.

Rnd 6: join blue cotton to last st of previous rnd. 3 ch, 1 tr in first tr of previous rnd, 2 tr, 2 tr in next st, *1 ch, miss 1 st, 2 tr in next st, 2 tr, 2 tr in next st*, rep from * to * twelve more times, finish with 1 ch, miss 1 st, ss in 3rd ch of t-ch

Rnd 7: 1 ch, *5 dc, 2 dc (inserting hook under ch on previous rnd)*, rep from * to * eleven more times, ss in first dc to join

Rnd 8: 2 ch, 1 tr in base of ch, 1 tr, (1 tr,1 htr) in next st, 1 ch, miss 1 st, *(1 htr, 1 tr) in next st, 1 tr, (1 htr, 1 tr) in next st, 1 ch, miss 1 st*, repeat from * to * twelve more times, ss in the 2nd ch of t-ch to join

In next rnd to finish off, work all the slip stitches by inserting hook under the top of the htr or tr in the row below.

Rnd 9: *ss in htr, ss in 3 tr, skip 1 htr, 1dc in st skipped in Rnd 8*, repeat from * to * thirteen more times, ss in first ss to join

Fasten off and weave in ends.

HEAD

Do the first rnd by crocheting both sides of chain and crochet next rows continuously, in off-white cotton, without closing previous rnd.

Use a marker to indicate the start of each round, moving it as the work progresses.

Rnd 1: 8 ch, 5 htr in 3rd ch from hook, 5 htr, 6 htr in last ch, rotate fabric and (working up the other side of the ch) 5 htr

Rnd 2: *2 htr in each of next 6 sts, 5 htr*, rep from * to *

Rnd 3: 2 htr, *2 htr in each of next 4 sts, 9 htr, 2 htr in each of next 4 sts, 7 htr

First horn: *10 ch, 1 htr in 3rd ch from hook, 3 htr, 4 dc, 1 dc in base of ch*, miss 2 htr, 6 tr in next st (making top of head)

Second horn: 1 dc in next st, repeat from * to *, ss in next st to join.

Fasten off and weave in ends.

Attach the head to the body using a blind stitch, keeping the stitches small.

TAIL

Using off-white cotton, skip four patterned shapes from Rnd 9, work in next dc: *6 ch, 1 htr in 3rd ch from hook, 2 htr, 1 dc, 1 dc in base of ch*, rep from * to * two more times.

Fasten off and weave in ends.

LEGS

Using brown cotton, 20 ch, miss three scalloped edge shapes from the tail, ss in next dc to join, 20 ch.

Row 1: 1 ch, 19 dc, 1 dc in Rnd 9 of Body, 19 dc down first ch

Fasten off and weave in ends.

Do the same for the other legs after the fifth scalloped edge.

HOOVES

Join blue cotton to the end of the leg with a ss, 1 ch, 10 dc in same st, ss in first dc to join. Fasten off and weave in yarn.

Repeat for the second, third and fourth legs.

EMBROIDERY

Using two strands of brown embroidery floss, embroider a rounded mouth shape in stem stitch, a slightly smaller nose above and two French knots for the eyes.

TIP

To make a mobile, crochet four sheep, swapping the colours of the central flower, legs and ring around the body. Thread white beads onto four nylon strands and attach a sheep to each end. Attach these hanging motifs to a simple white plastic ring. Make stars and flowers and stick them on using fabric glue.

Conversion Charts

Conversion Charts

YARN WEIGHTS

You will see that generally, a specific yarn weight or type is not provided. This is so that you can decide what type of yarn you wish to use to make each project. However, if you want some guidance on what to use, the hook size provided in the 'You will need list' gives an indication of which hook measurement is suitable. Then compare this with the hook size specified on the ball band of the yarn you'd like to use. If your band gives a larger hook size, the motifs will end up being larger than those in the book.

CROCHET TERMS

Be aware that crochet terms in the US are different from those in the UK. This can be confusing as the same terms are used to refer to different stitches under each system. The list here gives a translation of UK terms to US terms:

UK term	US term
slip stitch	slip stitch
double crochet	single crochet
half treble	half double crochet
treble	double crochet
double treble	treble crochet
triple treble	double treble crochet

CROCHET ABBREVIATIONS

ch	=	chain
st	=	stitch
ss	=	slip stitch
dc	=	double crochet
dc2tog	=	dc 2 together
htr	=	half treble
tr	=	treble
dtr	=	double treble
t-ch	=	turning chain
tr tr	=	triple treble
tog	=	together
foll	=	following
...	=	repeat instructions given between asterisks the number of times indicated
repl	=	replacing
rnd	=	round
rs	=	right side
ws	=	wrong side
rep	=	repeat

Conversion Charts

CROCHET HOOK SIZES

Crochet hooks come in a range of sizes, and the size of hook needed is directly related to the thickness of yarn being used. A fine yarn requires a small hook, while a thick yarn will need a much chunkier hook. There are two main sizing schemes for crochet hooks: the metric system (used in the UK and Europe) and the American system. The chart here lists the sizes available, with conversions for both systems.

Metric Size	American Size
2.00mm	B1
2.25mm	B1
2.50mm	C2
2.75mm	C2
3.00mm	D3
3.25mm	D3
3.50mm	E4
3.75mm	F5
4.00mm	G6
4.50mm	7
5.00mm	H8
5.50mm	I9
6.00mm	J10
6.50mm	K10½
7.00mm	-
8.00mm	L11
9.00mm	M/N13
10.00mm	N/P15
12.00mm	O16
15.00mm	P/Q
16.00mm	Q
19.00mm	S

Steel (or thread) crochet hooks are often used when crocheting with very fine yarns. Like other crochet hooks, there are also two main sizing schemes: the metric system (used in the UK and Europe) and the American system. The chart here lists the sizes available, with conversions for both systems.

Metric Size	American Size
2.5mm	US 0
2.2mm	US 2
2mm	US 4
1.8mm	US 6
1.5mm	US 8
1.3mm	US 10
1mm	US 12
0.75mm, 0.8mm	US 14
0.6mm	US 16

METRIC AND IMPERIAL MEASUREMENTS

These patterns have been created using metric measurements. Although imperial measurements appear in brackets after each metric measurement, for best results we recommend using the metric measurements provided.

About the Authors

Michelle Delpart and her daughters, Cécile and Sylvie, have embraced their family tradition that celebrates a love for all things handmade. With a seamstress grandmother and a knitting expert mother, it is only natural that they, too, see crafting as a way of life.

Dedicated to using natural materials, threads, yarns and fabrics within a little picture-postcard French town, they design products for their company, Emalisa, which they make in their workshop in Antananarivo, Madagascar. Michelle first discovered Madagascar twenty years ago. She was won over by the kindness of the Malagasy people and the grandeur of the landscape. She was also impressed by the ancestral know-how and needlework expertise of the women, so she decided to settle on the large island. She opened an embroidery and crocheting workshop fifteen years ago, with Cécile and Sylvie as partners.

By encouraging and supporting access to jobs for women, this workshop has taken on an important social and economic role in Antananarivo. Today it provides an income for around one hundred Malagasy families from underprivileged backgrounds. The women who work there are trained in the arts of crochet, embroidery, weaving and sewing so they can develop skills that can be used in a future career.

Fair trade is the core value for the company and it is especially important in a country where living conditions are difficult. The Emalisa workers enjoy benefits, such as access to medical care, regular meals and travel expenses. Local suppliers are selected based on their compliance with environmental standards, and the source of the products supplied is checked and controlled.

These beautiful creations are available to buy from the Emalisa website: www.emalisa.fr

Suppliers

UK AND EUROPE

EMALISA
4, Rue du Marché
33210 Langon
France
www.emalisa.fr

HOBBYCRAFT
www.hobbycraft.co.uk

STITCH CRAFT CREATE
Brunel House
Newton Abbot
Devon
TQ12 4PU, UK
www.stitchcraftcreate.co.uk

STYLECRAFT YARNS
PO Box 62
Keighley
West Yorkshire
BD21 1PP, UK
www.stylecraft-yarns.co.uk

WOOL WAREHOUSE
Longfield Road
Sydenham Industrial Estate
Leamington Spa
Warwickshire
CV31 1XB, UK
www.woolwarehouse.co.uk

AMERICA

HOBBY LOBBY STORES
www.hobbylobby.com

JOANN FABRIC AND CRAFT STORES
www.joann.com

Index

A DAVID & CHARLES BOOK
© Hachette Livre (Marabout) 2014
Originally published as Motifs au Crochet

First published in the UK and USA in 2015 by F&W Media International, Ltd
David & Charles is an imprint of F&W Media International, Ltd
Brunel House, Forde Close, Newton Abbot, TQ12 4PU, UK

F&W Media International, Ltd is a subsidiary of F+W Media, Inc
10151 Carver Road, Suite #200, Blue Ash, OH 45242, USA

A catalogue record for this book is available from the British Library.

ISBN-13: 978-1-4463-0575-1 paperback
ISBN-10: 1-4463-0575-9 paperback

ISBN-13: 978-1-4463-7088-9 PDF
ISBN-10: 1-4463-7088-7 PDF

ISBN-13: 978-1-4463-7087-2 EPUB
ISBN-10: 1-4463-7087-9 EPUB

Printed in China by RR Donnelley for:
F&W Media International, Ltd
Brunel House, Forde Close, Newton Abbot, TQ12 4PU, UK

10 9 8 7 6 5 4 3 2 1

Acquisitions Editor (UK): Sarah Callard
Desk Editor (UK): Charlotte Andrew
Technical explanations: Bernadette Baldelli
Pattern Checker (UK): Zoe Clements
Page make-up: Frédéric Voisin
Stylist: Aurélie Soligny
Photographer: Nathalie Carnet
Art Editor (UK): Anna Fazakerley
Production Manager (UK): Beverley Richardson

F+W Media publishes high quality books on a wide range of subjects.
For more great book ideas visit: www.stitchcraftcreate.co.uk

Layout of the digital edition of this book may vary depending on reader
hardware and display settings.